STORYBUILDING

A Guide To Structuring Oral Narratives

Peg Hutson-Nechkash

THINKING PUBLICATIONS® Eau Claire, WI
A Division of McKinley Companies, Inc.

ISBN 0-930599-63-2

Illustrations: Kris Madsen
Cover Design: Robert T. Baker
Printed in the United States of America

A Division of McKinley Companies, Inc.

P.O. Box 163
Eau Claire, WI 54702-0163
(715) 832-2488

ACKNOWLEDGMENTS

My sincere appreciation to the many people who have contributed to the completion of this book. First, the students, staff, and administration of the Dodgeville School District, from whom I have learned so much. Eve Bruce, Jeanette Jordan, and Jay Szalapski provided invaluable input and direction. My reviewers, Vicki Lord Larson, Emily Moore, Mary Ollinger, Peggy Reichardt, Caroline Rogers, Linda Schwartz, and Delores Kluppel Vetter, willingly shared their ideas and suggestions, for which I am grateful. Thanks also to Vivian Joubert for her expert technical editing. Special acknowledgment to Nancy McKinley for her unerring insights and remarkable attention. Final thanks must go to my family, especially my husband, John, and my parents, Tom and Betty Hutson, who never stopped believing in me.

Peg Hutson-Nechkash holds a Master of Science degree in Communication Disorders from the University of Wisconsin-Eau Claire, and the Certificate of Clinical Competence from the American Speech-Language-Hearing Association. Ms. Hutson-Nechkash is currently a speech-language pathologist for the Dodgeville School District in Dodgeville, Wisconsin.

CREDITS

The narrative examples on pages 5 and 6 are adapted from *Topics in Language Disorders*, Vol. 7, No. 1, pp. 62-64, with permission of Aspen Publishers, Inc., © December 1986.

The *Narrative Levels Analysis* on page 17 is adapted from **Communication Assessment and Intervention Strategies for Adolescents,** p. 297, V.L. Larson and N.L. McKinley, with permission of Thinking Publications, © 1987.

The *Suggested Books* on pages 43 and 44 are reprinted from **Topics in Language Disorders,** Vol. 7, No. 1, pp. 82-83, with permission of Aspen Publishers, Inc., © December 1986.

TABLE OF CONTENTS

Introduction 1

Assessment 11

Remediation... 29

    Familiarization 34

    Practice 45

    Critiquing... 85

    Generalization... 126

Bibliography 137

INTRODUCTION

INTRODUCTION

Recently, the focus in communication assessment and intervention has shifted from the sentence level to larger linguistic units termed *discourse*. Conversations and narrations are two types of discourse. There exists both similiarites and differences between narrations and conversations. "Both require a sense of purpose, the selection of relevant information, the clear and orderly exchange of this information, the ability to make necessary repairs, and the ability to assume the perspective of the listener or audience" (Roth, 1986, p. 22). Roth and Spekman (1986, as reported in Larson and McKinley, 1987) detail some of the differences between narrations and conversations:

1. Narrations have more extended or elaborated units of text than conversations.
2. Narrations are expected to have story markers (e.g., an introduction and closing) and an orderly presentation of events leading to a logical resolution.
3. Narrations carry the expectation that the speaker will engage in an oral monologue and that the listener's role can be more passive. More responsibility is placed on the speaker to be organized, coherent, and interesting. (p.11)

Assessment and intervention materials, which focus on speech acts and other pragmatic areas to address conversation skills, have proved invaluable to the speech-language pathologist. Additionally, there is a need for assessment and intervention materials to address narrative skills. Failure to achieve narrative skills at the expected age levels limits communicative competence in both academic and social domains (Stephens, 1987). Academically, narratives play a role in reading skills, in telling or writing stories, and in comprehending any story-based information. Content areas such as science, social studies, and health all include materials which contain a storyline. Socially, the ability to recount experiences and events from our lives is an important communication tool that we use daily. Life can be viewed as a series of events sequenced temporally (Stephens, 1987). Narrative discourse allows us to interpret and organize these events. Although narratives are an important source and means of communication, they are seldom considered in a speech-language diagnostic evaluation or remediation program. Too often, the speech-language pathologist is left with a lingering sense that something is wrong with this individual's communication system, but is unsure how to assess or provide therapy. Here are two examples, taken from the author's files, which demonstrate how communication can break down in a narrative:

> My sister went to the pep rally and I didn't, so I went, so I decided to make a little Sky Commander out of my Centurion. It broke today, when I was in Mrs. Vandre's. I'd rather buy one for $4.00. I want Grandpa to get those cows in the barn.

> I went up to Wal-Mart® and put something on lay-away. It's kind of like a horse. Then they keep it 'til when you want it off and stuff, so then when you get ready, when you get it off, when you have the money. Mine was only $5.00, cause I put some money on lay-away the first time. So my mom helped the first time...the first time I put something on lay-away. Put something on lay-away, Ms. Hutson.

The first narrative sample is from a boy, ten years of age. The second narrative sample is from a girl, nine years of age. In each instance, the child had a desire to communicate and a willing listener. Unfortunately, these students were not able to construct a narrative in a logical and appropriate manner. These preceding narrative samples are considered to be personal narratives, since they are based on true experiences. Sutton-Smith and Heath (1981) have identified three types of narratives:

1. Fictional Narratives-Fantasies
2. Personal Narratives-True experiences
3. Personal Fictions-Mixtures of fantasies and true experiences

THE ACQUISITION OF NARRATIVE SKILLS

Children's narratives have always played an important role in language development. Among a child's first narrations are the stories told when looking at picture books or retelling favorite stories. During the primary school years, narrations are evidenced in Show-and-Tell and Sharing Time. A child's narrative also plays a role in connecting home and school experiences. During the middle and high school years, a student's personal narrative may serve as the basis for writing tasks. Clearly, children who have difficulty structuring narratives would be handicapped throughout the school years (Scott, 1988).

When asked to make up a story, children will frequently begin the narration with "Once upon a time..." indicating that this more literary style has been incorporated into the child's repertoire. Children learn this literary style through repeated exposure to books and stories. Children also learn to narrate by hearing and reading stories. "Listening to and reading high-quality literature allows students to experience all the language components together and promotes narrative development" (Van Dongen and Westby, 1986, p.80).

Children acquire narration skills not only through exposure to well-formed stories, but also by practicing and developing these skills. Children as young as two or three years will relate stories to listeners (Kemper and Edwards, 1986). Van Dongen and Westby (1986) state, "Children's development of narrative discourse grows within the context of their daily lives, as they tell personal narratives about themselves and others and build their experiences and knowledge about the world" (p. 71).

The next two sections, *Levels of Narrative Development* and *Story Grammar Skills*, represent two perspectives for viewing narratives: a developmental sequence (i.e., Applebee, 1978) or a story grammar taxonomy (i.e., Stein and Glenn, 1979).

LEVELS OF NARRATIVE DEVELOPMENT

The acquisition of narrative skills seems to follow a developmental progression, with early developing skills providing the foundation for later acquired skills. Applebee (1978) has outlined six basic types of narrative structure, followed by four additional levels of narrative development, based on Piaget's levels of cognitive development (Ault, 1977). Examples of children's narratives are from Hedburg and Stoel-Gammon (1986).

TYPES OF NARRATIVE STRUCTURE

HEAPS - Heaps are the earliest prenarrative structure. These are collections of unrelated ideas. Children switch topics freely with no apparent connections between the utterances. The sentences are generally simple declarations, usually in the present or present progressive tenses (Westby, 1984). Cohesive techniques are not used. "Children who tell heap stories often do not appear to recognize that the characters on each page of picture books are the same characters" (Westby, 1984, p. 115). For example a child might say:

A dog is walking down the street. A cat is fighting the dog and a baby is crying. The baby is sleeping. The boy is playing on the swing. The man is laying down and the girl is jumping the jump rope. The lady is cooking chocolate chip cookies. A girl is going to the store. The man is going into the supermarket. The old man is fighting the other man. That's all. (Hedburg and Stoel-Gammon, 1986, p. 62)

APPROXIMATE AGE OF EMERGENCE   2 YEARS

SEQUENCES - Sequences represent the second stage of prenarrative development. The term *sequences* is confusing, since the elements of the stories are linked together by arbitrary commonalities but without a common characteristic. Sequence stories do include a macrostructure which involves a central character, topic, or setting. "The story elements are related to the central macrostructure on perceptual bonds" (Westby, 1984, p. 115). For example:

She lives with her dad. She lives with her mother. Grandma and Grandpa live together. And these three children live with their grandma. And these two animals live with them. And that's all. (Hedburg and Stoel-Gammon, 1986, p. 62)

APPROXIMATE AGE OF EMERGENCE   2 to 3 YEARS

PRIMITIVE NARRATIVES - Primitive narratives typify the next level of narrative development. Like the sequence stories, primitive narratives contain a macrostructure of a central character, topic, or setting. Unlike the sequences, the events in a primitive narrative follow from the central core. This main theme requires the child to interpret or predict events. "Children producing primitive narratives recognize and label facial expressions and body postures, and in their stories they make frequent reference to the associated feelings of the character "(Westby, 1984, p.117). Children at this level of narrative development do not always recognize the reciprocal causality between thoughts and events (Larson and McKinley, 1987). Cohesive techniques such as use of pronominals and reiteration of the main character's name may be used. These techniques link individual sentences to the major theme but generally not to each other. For example:

My dad, he went up to go to work. My mom stayed and sleep in. My two brothers, they went to go play with the toys. My dog, she went outside. My kitty cat came up and he tickled me and came up and started to meow. And then I started to cry because he bit me. And my brothers came runnin' in and Mike said, "What happened?" They said, "What happened?" "My kitty cat just bit me." So mom comes runnin' in and she said, "What happened? Oh, the kitty cat bit you. O.K." (Hedburg and Stoel-Gammon, 1986, p. 62)

APPROXIMATE AGE OF EMERGENCE   3 to 4 YEARS

UNFOCUSED CHAINS - Unfocused chains are the next level of narrative development. These stories contain no central character or topic. Unfocused chains present an actual sequence of events yet there is no consistency of character or theme. The events are linked

5

in logical or cause-effect relationships. Cohesive techniques of connecting words and propositions may appear. The conjunctions *and, but,* and *because* may also be used. This type of narrative structure is seldom produced by children, for as soon as cause-effect and sequential relationships appear, children will begin to tie the story elements to each other and to a central theme (Westby, 1984). For example:

> This man is walking. He saw a dog and a cat and he saw a girl, too, with the cat and the dog. He said, "Hello." He walked back and he said, "Brother, come here." So her grandmother walked up to her and said, "You wanna go dancing?" They went dancing. And so it was a slow dance. And then they went back. And then these two children came. And then first he said, "I'm not." And then he said, "What?" "I wanna go out to eat." So they went out to eat. (Hedburg and Stoel-Gammon, 1986, p. 63)

APPROXIMATE AGE OF EMERGENCE   **4 TO 4 1/2 YEARS**

FOCUSED CHAINS - Focused chains are comprised of a central character with a logical sequence of events. These chains describe a chain of events that take the form of a series of "adventures." There are central characters and a true sequence of events but the listeners must interpret the ending. Westby (1984) states, "...the characters' actions seldom lead to attainment of a goal; consequently, if no goal is perceived, then, in the child's thinking, there is no need for an end to the story, or, at least, the ending does not have to follow logically from the beginning" (p. 118). For example:

> Once upon a time there was a mother named Christie. And she had a husband named Tom. And they had some children named Heather and Christie. And then they had a boy named Ronnie. And the mother told the boy to go outside to play. And then the boy came in and said, "Mother, mother, our dog's outside and he's barking. I will go see. What are you barking at? I don't know what he was barking at, Tommy, Ronnie, Ronnie. I don't know what he was barking at. You go out there and see. He wants in. I'll go let him in. There, I let him in." (Hedburg and Stoel-Gammon, 1986, p. 63)

APPROXIMATE AGE OF EMERGENCE   **5 YEARS**

TRUE NARRATIVES - The level of true narratives represents the next stage of narrative development. True narratives adopt a consistent perspective focused on an incident in a story. There is a true plot, character development, and sequence of events. The presented problem, which is related to issues introduced in the beginning, is resolved in the end. Children may also perceive the relationship between attributes of characters and events. For example:

> One day there was a boy named Bobby and a girl named Sharon. They found a cat in their front yard and they brought it into the house. They fed the cat and they gave it some milk. They played and played with it and then a little while after a lady called and asked if anybody had seen her cat. And then they said that they had it at their house. And they brought it to the lady's house. And she gave them each five dollars for finding the cat and having them feed it and give it milk. (Hedburg and Stoel-Gammon, 1986, p. 64)

APPROXIMATE AGE OF EMERGENCE   **6 to 7 YEARS**

Children's narrative development does not end at seven years of age. Rather, children seem to lengthen and refine their narratives. The elements of the narratives also grow more complex as the child matures (Applebee, 1978).

7-11 YEARS OF AGE - At this level of development, children will now begin to summarize and categorize stories. Children may categorize stories subjectively or objectively. "Subjectively, the child may categorize or summarize a story as 'funny' or 'exciting' or 'sad.' Objectively, the child may summarize a story as rhyming or long. In either case, the child is capable of considering the entire story and placing it in a more general category" (Larson and McKinley, 1987, p. 100).

11-12 YEARS OF AGE - Children at this level of development are now capable of producing complex stories with multiple embedded narrative structures.

13-15 YEARS OF AGE - Adolescents who reach this level of development are now adept at analyzing stories. This analysis is often combined with evaluation of stories or elements of stories.

16 YEARS OF AGE TO ADULTHOOD - Individuals at this level of narrative development are now capable of more sophisticated analysis. When presented with a story, these individuals are now able to generalize about the story's meaning, formulate abstract statements about the message or theme of the story, and focus on their reaction to the story (Larson and McKinley, 1987).

STORY GRAMMAR SKILLS

Some stories produced by children may be best described using a set of rules to illustrate their underlying structure. A story grammar framework may then be utilized. "Story grammars are goal-based definitions of stories in which a major character, the protagonist, is motivated to achieve a goal through engaging in some type of goal-oriented action" (Hedburg and Stoel-Gammon, 1986, p. 64). A story grammar framework assists both the speaker and the listener in a narrative exchange. The use of a story grammar appears to represent the speaker's knowledge of narrative structure as well as allowing the listener to use a story grammar framework to assimilate the narrative input (Roth, 1986). While several different story grammars have been proposed, Stein and Glenn (1979) suggest that stories are comprised of a setting and one or more episodes. An episode includes an initiating event + an internal response + a plan + an attempt + a consequence + a reaction. If a story does include more than one episode, these episodes may be linked sequentially, temporally, or causally (Roth, 1986). Definitions for each of these story grammar components are listed below:

1. <u>Setting</u> statements introduce the main character(s) and describe the context of the story.
2. <u>Initiating events</u> induce the protagonist(s) to react in some way.
3. <u>Internal responses</u> describe the character's(s') thoughts, intentions, or emotional responses to the initiating events.
4. <u>Internal plans</u> are statements referring to the protagonist's(s') strategy for reaching the goal.
5. <u>Attempts</u> are made overtly by the protagonist(s) to obtain the goal.
6. <u>Consequences</u> are the outcome and indicate whether the attempts of the

protagonist(s) were successes or failures.

7. <u>Reactions</u> are descriptions of how the character(s) now feel, think, or respond emotionally.

This story grammar model does not characterize perfectly all stories. Rather, it provides a framework for viewing children's stories. Through repeated exposure to stories, most children develop adequate story grammar knowledge. A narrative produced by an adolescent should contain all seven of these components (Larson and McKinley, 1987). Story grammar analysis and narrative developmental levels allow us to evaluate and make judgments regarding an individual's ability to structure and produce an oral narrative. The next section will provide a description of some of the types of narrative disabilities shown by school-age children.

NARRATIVE DISABILITIES

Many students with language/learning disabilities also exhibit difficulty structuring oral narratives. Elementary school children may be producing narratives characteristic of much younger children. Language-impaired adolescents may not have reached the level of producing a true narrative. Instead, their narrative development may be limited to focused chains and primitive narratives.

Unfortunately, many children with language delays and disorders also experience difficulty with reading skills. Language-impaired children may also be reluctant to share and practice narratives with others. Therefore, these important sources of language stimulation may not be readily accessible.

In a study comparing spontaneously produced stories told by learning disabled students with those produced by their normally achieving peers, Roth and Spekman (1985) reported that the stories told by the learning disabled students were shorter, contained fewer descriptors, less detail, and substantially fewer complete episodes. Furthermore, the learning disabled students demonstrated less usage of response, plan and attempt statements, and were less likely to connect statements, as compared to their normally achieving peers. An important prerequisite in the generation of a spontaneous story is the ability to assume a character's perspective. The speaker must be able to perceive how a character in the story might feel, even though the speaker might feel different. This is especially true for stories in which a character's feelings or thoughts may not be explicitly stated. For language/learning disabled students, this awareness of an individual character's own thoughts and motivation seems to be slow in developing (Westby, 1985).

Norris and Brunig (1988) examined the narratives of one hundred and fifty good and poor readers in kindergarten and first grade. Their findings indicate that the poor readers produced stories that were shorter, contained fewer ideas, and included more irrelevant information. In addition, the poor readers were less likely to tie the story elements together and to link characters and events.

Westby (1984) has identified three patterns of difficulties in structuring oral narratives for language/learning disabled children:

1. Inefficient processing - Children with inefficient processing may be able to produce a narrative with an appropriate macrostructure. However, these students may

exhibit delayed responses, difficulty changing tasks, and slow retrieval of words. In addition, they may use vague, nonspecific vocabulary, and frequently need repetitions and cues.

2. Inadequate organization - These students may be characterized as possessing problems in planning. They may be able to answer questions appropriately about the characters' motivations and cause-effect relationships. However, their narratives are not organized in a logical, coherent manner. The narratives may only be sequential statements. These stories lack a theme or plot and may include irrelevant details.

3. Insufficient schema knowledge - These students also demonstrate problems in planning. They may not be aware that the pictures contained in a book present a story. They may describe each picture as a separate stimulus. Cause-effect and motivational relationships may not be perceived or correctly interpreted by these children.

NARRATION ANALYSIS

Speech-language pathologists working with school-age children are required by P.L. 94–142 to evaluate and assess linguistic functioning. Then, this information needs to be presented to a multidisciplinary team for decisions regarding placement and IEP development. To develop an overall profile of a child's language abilities, narrative analysis is vital. "Narrative analysis is one of the most valuable skills a language clinician can possess" (Hedburg and Stoel-Gammon, 1986, p. 58). Narrative analysis is best done using informal assessment procedures, since standardized testing methods seldom detect narrative disabilities (Westby, 1984). "Short answers to standardized test questions do not tax cognitive organization and formulation skills to the degree that classroom and social encounters frequently demand" (Simon, 1985, p. 205). The following section, entitled *Assessment*, provides guidelines for collecting narrative samples, assessment forms to evaluate narrative and story grammar development, and interpretative information. However, caution should be exercised when using the *STORYBUILDING* *Assessment* and *Remediation* sections with culturally different individuals.

In recent years, there have been increasing numbers of school-age children from multi-cultural backgrounds. While stories produced by children from many cultures seem to follow a consistent organizational structure, speech-language pathologists need to be sensitive to the nature of narratives in other cultures (Westby, 1989). For example, the attributes of certain characters in some children's stories, such as the wise owl or the curious cat, seem to be culturally bound. Therefore, the speech-language pathologist needs to exert care when doing narrative assessment and intervention with culturally different students. "Speech-language pathologists should recognize that using the middle-class English-speaking child as the norm is no longer adequate for the language assessment of minority children" (Kayser, 1989, p. 226).

ASSESSMENT

ASSESSMENT

Because a child's ability to logically structure and relate a personal narrative is such a critical skill, the speech-language pathologist must have adequate diagnostic information. Therefore, two assessment forms are included as measures of a child's ability to logically structure and relate a narrative. These assessment forms are entitled: *Narrative Levels Analysis* and *Story Grammar Assessment*.

The *Narrative Levels Analysis* is based on Applebee's (1978) developmental narrative sequence arranged according to Jean Piaget's periods of cognitive development (Ault, 1977). The *Levels of Story Grammar Development* (see page 18) are based on Glenn and Stein's (1980) story grammar taxonomy for the acquisition of story structure. A *Narrative Levels Analysis* or *Story Grammar Assessment* form should be completed for each narrative sample collected. The purpose of this task is to make judgments regarding the child's level of narrative development, not to capture the story. These forms may be used as part of an initial diagnostic evaluation or to measure progress for a three year re-evaluation or end of the year assessment. On pages 20-26, sample *Story Grammar Assessment* forms have been completed for each level of story grammar development.

These assessment measures are appropriate for individuals who have been determined to have a mean length of utterance of three words or more (Hedburg and Stoel-Gammon, 1986). Although the assessment measures were designed to be used with individuals possessing a MLU ≥ 3.0, there are some individuals for whom a particular assessment form would be more appropriate. The *Narrative Levels Analysis* is most appropriate for assessing the narrative development of individuals with limited verbal skills. Specifically, individuals with limited verbal skills include preschool and lower elementary school-age language-impaired children, children with hearing impairments, mentally retarded students, and adults with aphasia (Hedburg and Stoel-Gammon, 1986). The *Story Grammar Assessment* is better suited for the assessment of children who are producing stories with the focused chain or true narrative structure (Westby, 1984). The narrative levels of summarization, analysis, and generalization may best capture the narratives produced by adolescents.

For either type of analyses, it is recommended that a minimum of <u>three</u> samples of the child's narrations be collected and analyzed to obtain a clearer picture of a child's true ability. To aid in assessment, the examiner may wish to collect, from the child, one narrative sample from each of the following categories:

1. Personal experience narrative
2. TV program, movie, or book summary
3. Fictional story

A personal experience narrative can be collected by asking the child to tell about a family trip, vacation, a funny incident, or any occurrence in which the child is a main character. The second category of narratives can be obtained by feigning ignorance of a book the child has read or a TV program or movie the child has seen. The student can also be asked to tell the story that he/she sees in a Viewmaster⁽ that the examiner cannot see. A third method is to show the student a short video, puppet show, or cartoon and ask the child to retell the story to a person who was not present when the stimulus was being shown (Emily Moore, Personal Communication, 1989).

When collecting a fictional story from a child, instruct the child to "...tell a story like you would read in a book." This directive alerts the child to switch to a more literary style of language (Westby, 1984). It is also important to look at the amount of structure that is provided when a child is asked "to tell a story." One way to consider the structure provided is to imagine a continuum where the poles represent no structure provided as opposed to a high degree of structure. Most narratives considered for assessment will fall somewhere between the two extremes, depending on the individual's linguistic ability and willingness to communicate. We can classify the amount of structure accordingly:

Table 2.1   Amount of Narrative Structure

NO STRUCTURE		MEDIUM AMOUNT OF STRUCTURE		HIGH DEGREE OF STRUCTURE
The child chooses the topic and formulates a narrative	The child is given a topic and is asked to tell a story	The child is given an action picture with obvious characters and surroundings	The child is given a starting sentence containing the setting, characters, and an initiating event and is asked to complete the story	The child is told a story, or given sequence cards, and is asked to reformulate that story

In the initial assessment of a child, a medium amount of structure should be provided when asking a child to formulate a narrative. Depending on how well the child completes the task with some structure, more or less structure may be provided for subsequent narration assessment tasks. Children with limited verbal ability and/or a reluctance to communicate may benefit from a high degree of structure. "The instruction to make up a story when no stimulus material is provided is the most demanding for the child, because all schemas must be evoked and organized rather than simply recognized" (Westby, 1984, p.121). Individuals with more fully developed linguistic skills may be able to produce a true narrative with little or no structure provided. If the student is able to produce a narrative at an age-appropriate level, with no additional structure provided, then that student probably does not need this program. Therefore, when using the assessment procedures, the examiner should indicate the amount and type of structure provided, since these variables will influence the child's narrative production. When providing additional structure to a child in a diagnostic evaluation, one should bear in mind the child's level of familiarity and experience with the given stimulus. Familiar stories told in a familiar style ("Once upon a time...") seem to elicit more well-formed stories than unfamiliar items.

Keep in mind that language is most meaningful when it is purposeful. While a request from a speech-language pathologist to "make up a story" may seem very purposeful to some, it probably does not seem like a very functional or necessary task to a child. Optimally, narratives for assessment are best obtained when the child has a purpose for communicating within a naturalistic context.

The last page of the *Assessment* section includes a supplemental assessment form entitled *Style of Narration Assessment*. This form may be completed for each narrative sample collected from the student or following the analysis of several samples from a student. The questions on this form pertain to the manner in which the narrative was told. The information gathered from this form, while subjective, will be beneficial to parents and teachers, as well as to the speech-language pathologist.

INTERPRETATION

Once the speech-language pathologist has analyzed the student's narrative and story grammar development, decisions then need to be made as to whether or not this child is a candidate for language intervention. To achieve the most accurate normative data, it is recommended that the speech-language pathologist establish norms based upon the local population. The speech-language pathologist has the option of using the following information to interpret scores.

NARRATIVE LEVELS ANALYSIS

The *Narrative Levels Analysis* on page 17, provides an approximate age of emergence for each level of narrative structure. Students whose narrative language samples are consistently two to three years delayed, compared to chronological age, may benefit from language intervention.

STORY GRAMMAR ASSESSMENT

Although normative data for the *Story Grammar Assessment* are not yet available, the examiner can make judgments regarding the student's story-telling and narrative abilities. Through the use of the *Story Grammar Assessment*, the examiner can determine the structural elements that are present in the child's speech and those that have not yet been demonstrated or acquired by the child. As previously reported, the *Story Grammar Assessment* is best suited for children who are producing stories with the focused chain or true narrative structure (Westby, 1984). This would then suggest a minimum level of linguistic development comparable to a normally developing child of five to six years of age. The final question on the *Story Grammar Assessment* form corresponds to a story grammar structure that is generally observed in normally developing children of eleven to twelve years of age (Gmeiner Heinrich, 1989). This would suggest that between the ages of five and twelve years, normally developing children are in the process of developing and mastering these story grammar skills. Following the analysis of a story with the *Story Grammar Assessment*, the examiner can then determine the percentage of story grammar structures present in the child's language. These percentages can then be compared with the information in Table 2.2 to determine the level of story grammar development.

Table 2.2   Level of Story Grammar Development

12/12	100%	Level 7	Interactive Episode
11/12	92%	Level 6	Complex Episode
10/12	83%	Level 6	Complex Episode
9/12	75%	Level 5	Complete Episode
8/12	67%	Level 5	Complete Episode
7/12	58%	Level 4	Abbreviated Episode
6/12	50%	Level 4	Abbreviated Episode
5/12	42%	Level 3	Reactive Sequence
4/12	33%	Level 3	Reactive Sequence
3/12	25%	Level 2	Action Sequence
2/12	17%	Level 1	Descriptive Sequence
1/12	8%	Pre-Level 1	
0/12	0%	Pre-Level 1	

Children whose analyses reflect more than one level of development may be transitioning to a higher level of development. (See page 18 for a description of the seven levels of development.) It is also conceivable that a collected narrative language sample was not truly representative of the child's language. Therefore, further assessment would be warranted. Students may also be selected for intervention if the analyses of their stories reveal a significant number of NO responses. Children older than twelve years whose scores fall below 70% may be considered for further assessment and/or remediation. This minimum competency score of 70% was chosen, since "...thirty percent...[marked as NO] approximates two standard deviations below the mean on standardized tests" (Larson and McKinley, 1987, p. 109).

STYLE OF NARRATION ASSESSMENT

Through the use of the *Style of Narration Assessment*, the speech-language pathologist can develop a more comprehensive picture of the child's narrative abilities. While using this form, the following two points should be considered: 1. This assessment form is to be used with individuals who have reached the level of producing a true narrative; and 2. Story narratives, as compared to personal narratives, contain fewer pauses, repetitions, and false starts (Westby, 1984). On the *Style of Narration Assessment* as well, it is recommended that 70% be used as a guideline for the selection of candidates for remediation.

Included in the remainder of the *Assessment* section are the following:

1. Narrative Levels Analysis
2. Story Grammar Assessment
3. Levels of Story Grammar Development
4. Sample Story Grammar Assessment Forms
5. Style of Narration Assessment

NARRATIVE LEVELS ANALYSIS

NAME: _____ DATE: _____

AGE: _____ EXAMINER: _____

DIRECTIONS: Place check marks to reflect the highest level of narrative development for formulated and reformulated tasks.

Cognitive Period	Approximate "Normal" Age of Emergence	Mode of Organization	Tasks	
			Formulated	Reformulated
Pre-operations	2 years	Heaps		
	2 to 3 years	Sequences		
	3 to 4 years	Primitive narratives		
	4 to $4\frac{1}{2}$ years	Unfocused chains		
	5 years	Focused chains		
	6 to 7 years	Narratives		
Concrete	7 to 11 years	Summarization		
	11 to 12 years	Complex stories		
Formal	13 to 15 years	Analysis		
	16 years to adulthood	Generalization		

Description of formulated task: _____

Description of reformulated task: _____

Comments: _____

_____

_____

Adapted with permission from: *Communication Assessment and Intervention Strategies for Adolescents.* V.L. Larson and N. L. McKinley, Thinking Publications, Eau Claire, WI, 1987.

STORYBUILDING

LEVELS OF STORY GRAMMAR DEVELOPMENT

Glenn and Stein (1980) have suggested a developmental taxonomy for the acquisition of story grammar skills. Seven different levels have been identified ranging in complexity from simplest to most complex. Each level contains all the components of the previous levels with one additional component added. Examples of stories which illustrate each of these seven levels, with completed *Story Grammar Assessment* forms, are provided on pages 20-26.

Level 1 DESCRIPTIVE SEQUENCE

This story is comprised of descriptions of characters, surroundings, and usual actions of the characters. No causal relationships or sequences of events are present.

Level 2 ACTION SEQUENCE

This story consists of events in a chronological order but no causal relationships exist.

Level 3 REACTIVE SEQUENCE

This story does contain a causal relationsip in that certain changes automatically cause other changes. There is no evidence of goal-directed behavior.

Level 4 ABBREVIATED EPISODE

At this level, a goal is implied even though it may not be stated explicitly. This story contains either an event statement with a consequence or an internal response with a consequence. The actions of the characters seem to be purposeful, though not as well thought out as in successive stages.

Level 5 COMPLETE EPISODE

This story contains an entire goal-oriented behavior sequence. A consequence is required as well as two of the following three components: Initiating Event, Internal Response, Attempt.

Level 6 COMPLEX EPISODE

This level is an elaboration of the complete episode, with an additional partial or complete incident embedded in the episode. A story at this level could also contain multiple plans which are used to achieve the goal. Either one of these factors or both must be present.

Level 7 INTERACTIVE EPISODE

The interactive episode is the highest level. This story contains two characters with separate goals and actions that influence the actions of the other.

STORY GRAMMAR ASSESSMENT

NAME: _____

DATE: _____

Degree of structure provided:
- ___ No additional structure
- ___ Medium amount of structure
- ___ High degree of structure

Collect a narrative from the student. (See pages 7-8 for definitions.)

_____

1. IS A SETTING GIVEN?	YES	NO
2. ARE THE CHARACTERS DESCRIBED?	YES	NO
3. ARE THE EVENTS PRESENTED SEQUENTIALLY?	YES	NO
4. IS THERE A CAUSAL RELATIONSHIP BETWEEN EVENTS?	YES	NO
5. IS THERE AN INITIATING EVENT (IE)?	YES	NO
6. IS A GOAL PRESENT?	YES	NO
7. IS THERE A CONSEQUENCE?	YES	NO
8. IS AN INTERNAL RESPONSE (IR) PRESENT?	YES	NO
9. IS THERE AN ATTEMPT TO ATTAIN THE GOAL?	YES	NO
10. ARE MULTIPLE PLANS USED TO MEET THE GOAL?	YES	NO
11. IS A PARTIAL OR COMPLETE EPISODE EMBEDDED IN THE EPISODE?	YES	NO
12. ARE THERE TWO CHARACTERS WITH SEPARATE GOALS AND ACTIONS THAT INFLUENCE THE ACTIONS OF THE OTHER?	YES	NO

Number of YES Responses _____ ÷ 12 x 100 = _____ %

LEVEL OF STORY GRAMMAR DEVELOPMENT _____

Comments _____

_____

_____

STORYBUILDING

SAMPLE STORY GRAMMAR ASSESSMENT

Her mom took her at the zoo. She sees a monkey and she sees a giraffe. Now she went to a cage of lions. Now she comes to a place where a person sells balloons and stuff. Sometimes she sees elephants and stuff. She saw deers. Now she sees penguins. Then she went to a lake with ducks in it.

1.	IS A SETTING GIVEN?	(YES)	NO
2.	ARE THE CHARACTERS DESCRIBED?	(YES)	NO
3.	ARE THE EVENTS PRESENTED SEQUENTIALLY?	YES	(NO)
4.	IS THERE A CAUSAL RELATIONSHIP BETWEEN EVENTS?	YES	(NO)
5.	IS THERE AN INITIATING EVENT (IE)?	YES	(NO)
6.	IS A GOAL PRESENT?	YES	(NO)
7.	IS THERE A CONSEQUENCE?	YES	(NO)
8.	IS AN INTERNAL RESPONSE (IR) PRESENT?	YES	(NO)
9.	IS THERE AN ATTEMPT TO ATTAIN THE GOAL?	YES	(NO)
10.	ARE MULTIPLE PLANS USED TO MEET THE GOAL?	YES	(NO)
11.	IS A PARTIAL OR COMPLETE EPISODE EMBEDDED IN THE EPISODE?	YES	(NO)
12.	ARE THERE TWO CHARACTERS WITH SEPARATE GOALS AND ACTIONS THAT INFLUENCE THE ACTIONS OF THE OTHER?	YES	(NO)

Number of YES Responses ___2___ ÷ 12 x 100 = ___17___ %

LEVEL OF STORY GRAMMAR DEVELOPMENT _Level 1 Descriptive Sequence_

Comments _____

_____

_____

SAMPLE STORY GRAMMAR ASSESSMENT

I get up in the morning at 6:30. My mom gets up first. She wakes me up, then she wakes up my brother. Then I get dressed. My mom makes eggs for me, sometimes. Sometimes, I eat cereal. I make the toast. After I get done eating, I go out to wait for the bus.

1. IS A SETTING GIVEN? **(YES)** NO

2. ARE THE CHARACTERS DESCRIBED? **(YES)** NO

3. ARE THE EVENTS PRESENTED SEQUENTIALLY? **(YES)** NO

4. IS THERE A CAUSAL RELATIONSHIP BETWEEN EVENTS? YES **(NO)**

5. IS THERE AN INITIATING EVENT (IE)? YES **(NO)**

6. IS A GOAL PRESENT? YES **(NO)**

7. IS THERE A CONSEQUENCE? YES **(NO)**

8. IS AN INTERNAL RESPONSE (IR) PRESENT? YES **(NO)**

9. IS THERE AN ATTEMPT TO ATTAIN THE GOAL? YES **(NO)**

10. ARE MULTIPLE PLANS USED TO MEET THE GOAL? YES **(NO)**

11. IS A PARTIAL OR COMPLETE EPISODE EMBEDDED IN THE EPISODE? YES **(NO)**

12. ARE THERE TWO CHARACTERS WITH SEPARATE GOALS AND ACTIONS THAT INFLUENCE THE ACTIONS OF THE OTHER? YES **(NO)**

Number of YES Responses ___3___ ÷ 12 x 100 = ___25___ %

LEVEL OF STORY GRAMMAR DEVELOPMENT _Level 2 Action Sequence_

Comments _____

_____

_____

SAMPLE STORY GRAMMAR ASSESSMENT

Last summer, when I went to visit my grandpa, there was a fire at the house next door. My grandpa called the fire department. Pretty soon, the fire trucks came. Then the police came, too. The ambulance came, too. It was just a little fire. Nobody was hurt.

1. IS A SETTING GIVEN? **(YES)** NO

2. ARE THE CHARACTERS DESCRIBED? **(YES)** NO

3. ARE THE EVENTS PRESENTED SEQUENTIALLY? **(YES)** NO

4. IS THERE A CAUSAL RELATIONSHIP BETWEEN EVENTS? **(YES)** NO

5. IS THERE AN INITIATING EVENT (IE)? YES **(NO)**

6. IS A GOAL PRESENT? YES **(NO)**

7. IS THERE A CONSEQUENCE? YES **(NO)**

8. IS AN INTERNAL RESPONSE (IR) PRESENT? YES **(NO)**

9. IS THERE AN ATTEMPT TO ATTAIN THE GOAL? YES **(NO)**

10. ARE MULTIPLE PLANS USED TO MEET THE GOAL? YES **(NO)**

11. IS A PARTIAL OR COMPLETE EPISODE EMBEDDED IN THE EPISODE? YES **(NO)**

12. ARE THERE TWO CHARACTERS WITH SEPARATE GOALS AND ACTIONS THAT INFLUENCE THE ACTIONS OF THE OTHER? YES **(NO)**

Number of YES Responses ___4___ ÷ 12 x 100 = ___33___ %

LEVEL OF STORY GRAMMAR DEVELOPMENT ___Level 3 Reactive Sequence___

Comments _____

_____

_____

SAMPLE STORY GRAMMAR ASSESSMENT

One time, my dad was painting the house. He was painting it brown. He climbed up the ladder. Then his foot slipped on the ladder and he dropped the pail with the paint in it. I was standing by the ladder and I got paint all over me. It was in my hair and on my clothes.

---

1. IS A SETTING GIVEN?   (YES)   NO

2. ARE THE CHARACTERS DESCRIBED?   (YES)   NO

3. ARE THE EVENTS PRESENTED SEQUENTIALLY?   (YES)   NO

4. IS THERE A CAUSAL RELATIONSHIP BETWEEN EVENTS?   (YES)   NO

5. IS THERE AN INITIATING EVENT (IE)?   (YES)   NO

6. IS A GOAL PRESENT?   (YES)   NO

7. IS THERE A CONSEQUENCE?   (YES)   NO

8. IS AN INTERNAL RESPONSE (IR) PRESENT?   YES   (NO)

9. IS THERE AN ATTEMPT TO ATTAIN THE GOAL?   YES   (NO)

10. ARE MULTIPLE PLANS USED TO MEET THE GOAL?   YES   (NO)

11. IS A PARTIAL OR COMPLETE EPISODE EMBEDDED IN THE EPISODE?   YES   (NO)

12. ARE THERE TWO CHARACTERS WITH SEPARATE GOALS AND ACTIONS THAT INFLUENCE THE ACTIONS OF THE OTHER?   YES   (NO)

Number of YES Responses ___7___ ÷ 12 x 100 = ___58___ %

LEVEL OF STORY GRAMMAR DEVELOPMENT _Level 4 Abbreviated Episode_

Comments _____

_____

_____

SAMPLE STORY GRAMMAR ASSESSMENT

Sally woke up one beautiful, sunny morning. Sally looked out her window and saw a beautiful rainbow. Sally had always heard stories that at the end of the rainbow there was a pot of gold. She knew the end of the rainbow was far away and that her parents would be upset if she went looking for the pot of gold. Sally had to make the decision whether she should go or should not go. Sally made the decision to go.

Sally left her home and walked for miles and miles trying to find the end of the rainbow. Unfortunately, she got lost in the woods. Sally didn't know where to go or what to do. She was very scared and upset. Night was coming. She sat by a tree and wondered what was going to happen. She wanted to go home. Soon, she fell asleep.

The next morning, Sally woke up. She was cold and wet. She wandered around the woods, trying to find her way home. She tried to remember how she had come the day before. Finally, her parents found her. Sally decided that she would never go out in the woods alone again.

---

1. IS A SETTING GIVEN?   (YES)   NO

2. ARE THE CHARACTERS DESCRIBED?   (YES)   NO

3. ARE THE EVENTS PRESENTED SEQUENTIALLY?   (YES)   NO

4. IS THERE A CAUSAL RELATIONSHIP BETWEEN EVENTS?   (YES)   NO

5. IS THERE AN INITIATING EVENT (IE)?   (YES)   NO

6. IS A GOAL PRESENT?   (YES)   NO

7. IS THERE A CONSEQUENCE?   (YES)   NO

8. IS AN INTERNAL RESPONSE (IR) PRESENT?   (YES)   NO

9. IS THERE AN ATTEMPT TO ATTAIN THE GOAL?   (YES)   NO

10. ARE MULTIPLE PLANS USED TO MEET THE GOAL?   YES   (NO)

11. IS A PARTIAL OR COMPLETE EPISODE EMBEDDED IN THE EPISODE?   YES   (NO)

12. ARE THERE TWO CHARACTERS WITH SEPARATE GOALS AND ACTIONS THAT INFLUENCE THE ACTIONS OF THE OTHER?   YES   (NO)

Number of YES Responses ___9___ ÷ 12 x 100 = ___75___ %

LEVEL OF STORY GRAMMAR DEVELOPMENT _Level 5 Complete Episode_

24

SAMPLE STORY GRAMMAR ASSESSMENT

One time last summer, I went swimming in Lake Wissota with my friend MaryAnne. We were swimming off the dock at my house. Actually, I was swimming and MaryAnne was sitting on the dock. MaryAnne hasn't gone swimming since she was about six years old. When she was six, she was swimming and she swam to a real deep part, over her head. She couldn't swim back to the shore. She was really afraid. She kept going under the water. Finally, her brother saw her and saved her. So since then, MaryAnne doesn't like to swim.

Anyway, on this day, I was swimming and I found something in the sand on the bottom of the lake. It was a box buried in the sand. I wanted to open the box and see what was inside. I kept diving down to the bottom and pushing the sand away but I couldn't lift the box. It was buried too deep in the sand. I called MaryAnne to come and help me. She didn't want to go in the water but I talked her into it. Together, we kept pulling on the box. We tried for a long time but we couldn't move the box. We were so tired we had to stop. All that night we tried to imagine what was in the box. The next day we went back down to the lake to look for the box. Of course, MaryAnne didn't want to go in the water so I went by myself. I looked everywhere but I couldn't find the box. I thought I knew where the box was buried but I couldn't find it. MaryAnne even came in the lake to look for the box. We looked for two days but we never found the box again. Maybe the box got covered by sand again or we forgot where it was. We are going to look again, next summer, for that box.

---

1. IS A SETTING GIVEN? — (YES) NO

2. ARE THE CHARACTERS DESCRIBED? — (YES) NO

3. ARE THE EVENTS PRESENTED SEQUENTIALLY? — (YES) NO

4. IS THERE A CAUSAL RELATIONSHIP BETWEEN EVENTS? — (YES) NO

5. IS THERE AN INITIATING EVENT (IE)? — (YES) NO

6. IS A GOAL PRESENT? — (YES) NO

7. IS THERE A CONSEQUENCE? — (YES) NO

8. IS AN INTERNAL RESPONSE (IR) PRESENT? — (YES) NO

9. IS THERE AN ATTEMPT TO ATTAIN THE GOAL? — (YES) NO

10. ARE MULTIPLE PLANS USED TO MEET THE GOAL? — YES (NO)

11. IS A PARTIAL OR COMPLETE EPISODE EMBEDDED IN THE EPISODE? — (YES) NO

12. ARE THERE TWO CHARACTERS WITH SEPARATE GOALS AND ACTIONS THAT INFLUENCE THE ACTIONS OF THE OTHER? — YES (NO)

Number of YES Responses ___10___ ÷ 12 x 100 = ___83___ %

LEVEL OF STORY GRAMMAR DEVELOPMENT _Level 6 Complex Episode_

25

SAMPLE STORY GRAMMAR ASSESSMENT

Once there was a man who lived alone in the forest. He didn't want to live around other people. He was a gentle man who was trusted by the animals of the forest. During the spring, summer, and fall seasons, the man would collect berries, catch fish, and grow food. He would store the food for the long, cold winter.

One day, the man went out in the woods to find some blueberries. He walked a long way to find the berries. When he returned to his cabin, everything was a mess. Jars, cans, and sacks of food were tipped over and spilled on the floor. There were fruits and vegetables everywhere. The man did not know who could have done this. There were no other people around and the animals never went inside his cabin. The man cleaned up his cabin and then went outside. As he stepped out of the cabin, he realized that the forest was silent. No birds were singing and no squirrels scurried by. The man knew immediately that something was wrong.

On a hill overlooking the cabin sat a hungry watchful fox. He saw the man go back into the cabin. The fox slowly made his way down the hill towards the cabin. Inside the cabin, the man took out an old rifle. It was covered with dust. Carefully, the man dusted off the rifle and began to load it with shells. At that moment, the vicious fox stalked angrily outside the cabin. The man slowly opened the cabin door and stepped outside. He saw the fox. The man quickly raised his rifle, pointed it at the tallest tree, and fired. The noise frightened the fox, who turned and ran back up the hill to watch the man. The man stood there a long time and finally went inside the cabin. The man was afraid. He knew that he had frightened off the fox for now, but he also knew that the fox would return soon.

---

1. IS A SETTING GIVEN?	(YES)	NO
2. ARE THE CHARACTERS DESCRIBED?	(YES)	NO
3. ARE THE EVENTS PRESENTED SEQUENTIALLY?	(YES)	NO
4. IS THERE A CAUSAL RELATIONSHIP BETWEEN EVENTS?	(YES)	NO
5. IS THERE AN INITIATING EVENT (IE)?	(YES)	NO
6. IS A GOAL PRESENT?	(YES)	NO
7. IS THERE A CONSEQUENCE?	(YES)	NO
8. IS AN INTERNAL RESPONSE (IR) PRESENT?	(YES)	NO
9. IS THERE AN ATTEMPT TO ATTAIN THE GOAL?	(YES)	NO
10. ARE MULTIPLE PLANS USED TO MEET THE GOAL?	(YES)	NO
11. IS A PARTIAL OR COMPLETE EPISODE EMBEDDED IN THE EPISODE?	(YES)	NO
12. ARE THERE TWO CHARACTERS WITH SEPARATE GOALS AND ACTIONS THAT INFLUENCE THE ACTIONS OF THE OTHER?	(YES)	NO

Number of YES Responses ____12____ ÷ 12 x 100 = ____100____ %

LEVEL OF STORY GRAMMAR DEVELOPMENT _Level 7 Interactive Episode_

STYLE OF NARRATION ASSESSMENT

NAME: _____

DATE: _____

For each narrative sample collected, answer the following questions:

1. IS THE NARRATIVE GRAMMATICAL?   YES   NO

2. IS SUFFICIENT INFORMATION PRESENTED?   YES   NO

3. DOES THE LISTENER UNDERSTAND THE NARRATIVE
    WITHOUT ASKING QUESTIONS OF CLARIFICATION?   YES   NO

4. IS THE NARRATIVE PRESENTED IN A FLUENT MANNER
    (I.E., WITHOUT PAUSES, HESITATIONS, REVISIONS,
    OR FALSE STARTS)?   YES   NO

5. DOES THE SPEAKER TELL THE STORY WITHOUT EXHIBITING
    FRUSTRATION OR OBVIOUS DIFFICULTY?   YES   NO

6. IS ONE TOPIC PRESENTED (IF MORE THAN ONE TOPIC IS
    GIVEN, IS THERE A SMOOTH AND APPROPRIATE
    TRANSITION BETWEEN TOPICS)?   YES   NO

7. DO ALL THE STATEMENTS PERTAIN TO THE TOPIC(S)?   YES   NO

8. ARE PRECISE VOCABULARY TERMS USED (I.E., WITHOUT
    LOW INFORMATION WORDS LIKE *THINGS, STUFF*)?   YES   NO

9. ARE FACIAL AND BODY EXPRESSIONS APPROPRIATE TO
    THE STORY?   YES   NO

10. WAS THE TOPIC OF THE NARRATIVE APPROPRIATE FOR THE
    AUDIENCE?   YES   NO

Number of YES Responses _____ ÷ 10 x 100 = _____ %

DESCRIPTION OF NARRATIVE TASK _____

Comments _____

_____

_____

REMEDIATION

REMEDIATION

The purpose of the *STORYBUILDING* program is to improve children's narrative skills. This program was intended for use with upper elementary language and learning disabled students. Some aspects of this program are certainly suited for younger as well as older students.

Three principles underlie the *STORYBUILDING* program:

1. *Exposure to well-formed literature and a literary style of language.* Children who have been exposed to well-formed narratives and literature become aware that these books and stories have a pattern. They recognize that there is a continuity to stories. That is, the stories include a setting, characters, a problem, a goal, and a series of events leading to a resolution of the problem or a conclusion. Unfortunately, many of the stories and books currently being used in school, including basal readers, are not being written to facilitate narrative development. "The majority of basal reading texts make minimal use of folktales and well structured narratives" (Westby, 1984, p. 124).

2. *Development of metanarrative awareness.* Metanarrative awareness implies that the speaker has the ability to talk about the structure and elements of a narrative and to manipulate this structure intentionally. Skilled communicators are aware of the listener's needs and will present, in a logical manner, a narrative that includes the setting, characters, the time, and the events that occurred. The adept communicator may also be able to produce narrations with multiple character interactions and embedded episodes.

3. *Use of scaffolding techniques by the teacher or speech-language pathologist to aid in narrative construction.* Through the use of scaffolding techniques, children can be taught strategies for developing and producing narratives. "Scaffolding is the use of leading questions that help the speaker organize his or her story" (Page and Stewart, 1985, p. 25). Through the use of scaffolding, the language disordered child learns narrative skills in contexts where the more skilled language users provide the structure needed to complete a narrative. Gradually, this framework becomes internalized by the language-impaired child who is then able to generalize these skills without needing clarifying questions from adults.

As a rule, the scaffolding that is provided should be slightly more advanced than the child's level of development (Applebee and Langer, 1983). The scaffolding then serves as a means of helping the child to attain the next level of narrative development.

HOW TO USE THE
STORYBUILDING PROGRAM

The *STORYBUILDING* remediation program is comprised of four components: 1. Familiarization, 2. Practice, 3. Critiquing, and 4. Generalization.

Familiarization: This phase of the program emphasizes story grammar elements contained in children's literature. The goal of this familiarization process is to help the child recognize the story elements and use this schematic knowledge in the reformulation of stories.

Practice: This aspect of the *STORYBUILDING* program provides activities to build narrative skills. Through the use of sequence picture cards, story reformulations, story starters, and story frames, the students practice constructing narrations. As the students practice the production of narrations, it is also important to include the third phase, critiquing.

Critiquing: The critiquing activities should be done along with the practice activities. This aspect reinforces the child's schematic knowledge by making judgments regarding the quality of other narrations.

Generalization: The last component stresses the generalization of the child's schematic knowledge across settings. Application of narrative knowledge to the child's written language is also addressed.

The information and activities in this book have been arranged in discrete sections. However, each of the four components, *Familiarization, Practice, Critiquing,* and *Generalization* emphasizes skills that are used throughout the program. For example, the *Familiarization* phase uses children's literature to develop schematic knowledge. Reading high quality children's literature to language delayed/disordered students would be an appropriate therapy activity at any time during the use of this program. The *Practice* and *Critiquing* components go hand-in-hand. In each phase, the activities are arranged from easiest to most difficult. As a student develops the ability to produce a simple narrative, it would be appropriate to also critique one of the simpler narrations in the *Critiquing* section. These two activities can be easily accomplished in a 25-30 minute therapy session. However, the fourth component, *Generalization,* does require that the child be able to produce a narration without any additional structure provided. Figure 3.1 illustrates the interaction of these remediation components.

Figure 3.1   Interaction of Remediation Components

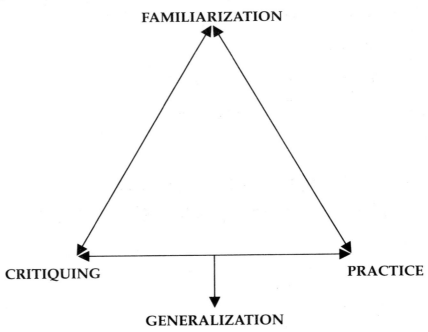

Ultimately, the goal of this program is for the student to be capable of producing logical and complete narratives. As a speech-language pathologist, teacher, aide, or parent, we have the opportunity to serve as language models for our language delayed/disordered children. For that reason, adult facilitators should regularly share their own personal experiences and stories with the children and allow time for the students to share their experiences.

FAMILIARIZATION

The first step of this program increases the students' familiarization with the elements basic to narrations. Relating to the continuum located on page 14, the first phase of the *STORYBUILDING* program emphasizes the production of narratives with a high degree of structure for the child. The goal of this step is two-fold: 1. To develop the child's ability to recognize these narrative elements in books and stories, and 2. To include these narrative elements in the reformulation of stories. Suggested, sample IEP goals are listed on pages 35-36. Using library books, stories from children's magazines, taped story books, fairy tales, folk tales, newspaper items, poems, and language experience stories, children learn to break down stories into their basic elements. On pages 37-38 are forms for capturing stories. While the assessment forms on pages 17 and 19 are intended to analyze a student's ability to formulate a story, these forms are intended as a means of breaking down a story into its component parts and then using the form to reformulate the story. The *Narration Elements* form on page 37 is intended for use with individuals possessing limited verbal abilities. The *Story Grammar Elements* form on page 38 is better suited for more skilled communicators as well as more complex stories. On page 39, the story grammar questions provided for the speech-language pathologist correspond to the taxonomy developed by Stein and Glenn (1979). The speech-language pathologist has the option to adjust the order in which the questions are asked.

When using books and stories that are not on tape, the speech-language pathologist should read the stories to the student. Since the books are being used for narrative skill building activities, the primary task should be listening, not reading (Larson and McKinley, 1987). After a book or story has been shared with the students, one of the basic forms is then completed. Initially, the speech-language pathologist may need to provide definitions and examples of the elements. In addition, not all of the components may be stated explicitly within the story. "In simple stories, some components may only be inferred from information actually contained in the story"(Page and Stewart, 1985, p. 18). As the speech-language pathologist and the students complete the form for each of the stories, discuss how crucial each of these elements is and how they mesh together to produce a well-formed story.

Stories are most easily recalled when:

1. The stories contain a high degree of redundancy (e.g., "Not by the hair of my chinny chin chin" from the *Three Little Pigs*).
2. The stories follow a familiar pattern (e.g., "Once upon a time...").
3. The events within the story are written in chronological order.
4. The stories are to be recalled orally rather than written.
5. The stories contain pictures, which the student uses when reformulating the story.
6. The child has knowledge of the story's topic.

Many individuals receiving speech and language services exhibit deficits and delays in several areas. Stories can then be chosen to address these other concerns. "If students have deficits in vocabulary, syntax, causality, time relationships, emotional understanding, and so on, literature can be selected that focuses on these components, presenting the components in a broader context"(Van Dongen and Westby, 1986, p. 80). To assist in selecting high quality literature, a list of children's books and stories has been included in this section. However, to maintain the student's motivation, some books and stories should be chosen which reflect the student's own interests.

Some individuals may need additional practice identifying the different elements of a story. Two practice activities are included on pages 40-42. These activities may also be used:

1. With a small or large group, generate a story. Write down all responses on a large sheet of paper. Cut the story apart into sentences and divide among the students. Designate different areas in the room to represent elements of the story. Ask the students to take their sentence to the appropriate area.

   Examples: "All character sentences kneel by the window."
   "All ending sentences sit by the pencil sharpener."

   Each individual is then asked to make three judgments about their sentence(s):

   a. Is my sentence in the right group?

   b. Is my sentence related to the topic?

   c. How does my sentence fit in order or sequence with the others in my group?

2. Another activity to help identify the elements of a story involves the use of color-coding. Assist the students to generate another story, writing down all responses, or use a published children's story. Copies are then made of the story and distributed to the students. Using different colored markers, the students mark those sentences that belong in the same category.

   Examples: "Draw a red line under the first event that occurred."
   "Put a blue circle around the ending."

3. For more capable students, write down all the sentences contained in the story, using a story book or story created by the students. Without the students' seeing the sentence, tape a sentence on each child's back. The children then need to ask questions of the others to determine the category in which their sentences belong:

   Examples: "Is this when the story happened?"
   "Do I have part of the plan?"

Included in this *Familiarization* section are the following:

1. *Narration Elements* form
2. *Story Grammar Elements - Student Copy*
3. *Story Grammar Elements - Clinician Copy*
4. Birthday Party Activity
5. Police Report Activity
6. Suggested Children's Books

SAMPLE I.E.P. GOALS

1. The student will be able to recognize and state, with 90% or greater accuracy, the narration elements of setting, characters, time, and beginning and ending events in a given story.

2. The student will be able to recognize and state, with 90% or greater accuracy, the story grammar elements of setting, characters, time, goal, plan, attempt, beginning and ending events, and results in a given story.

3. The student will be able to reformulate a given story, using the *Narration Elements* or *Story Grammar Elements* form, with 90% or greater accuracy.

NARRATION ELEMENTS

Name: _____   Date: _____

Title of story: _____

Source: _____

SETTING

CHARACTERS

TIME

EVENTS

Beginning

Ending

Using this form, retell the story.

STORYBUILDING

STORY GRAMMAR ELEMENTS
STUDENT COPY

Name: _____ Date: _____

Title of story: _____

Source: _____

What is the setting? _____

Who are the characters? _____

_____

When did this occur? _____

What happened first? _____

_____

What happened next? _____

_____

_____

Was this event caused by the first event? How? _____

_____

_____

_____

_____

What is the goal? _____

_____

What is the plan to reach this goal? _____

_____

_____

How was the plan attempted? _____

_____

_____

_____

What was the result? _____

_____

_____

How did it end? _____

_____

_____

Using this form, retell the story.

STORYBUILDING

STORY GRAMMAR ELEMENTS
CLINICIAN COPY

SETTING - Statements which introduce the main character(s) and describe the context of the story.

> What is the setting?
> Who are the characters?
> When did this occur?

INITIATING EVENT - An occurrence that induces the protagonist(s) to react in some way.

> What happened first?

INTERNAL RESPONSE - A statement which describes the character's(s') thoughts, intentions, or emotional responses to the initiating events.

> What happened next?
> Was this response caused by the first event? How?

INTERNAL PLAN - Statements referring to the protagonist's(s') strategy for reaching the goal.

> What is the goal?
> What is the plan to reach this goal?

ATTEMPT - Efforts made overtly by the protagonist(s) to obtain the goal.

> How was the plan attempted?

CONSEQUENCE - Direct results which indicate whether the attempts of the protagonist(s) were successes or failures.

> What was the result?

REACTION - Descriptions of how the character(s) now feels, thinks, or responds emotionally.

> How did it end?

A BIRTHDAY PARTY

Directions: Read the following story. Have the students identify the elements of setting, characters, time, and events in the story. Discuss how we can determine these components from the story. Have the students draw a picture of one of the story's elements.

In the summer, I had a birthday party at my house. I had four friends over: Mary, Kimberly, Tanya, and Amy. We played lots of games and cards. I had a birthday cake, too. It was a chocolate cake with white frosting and pink candles on top. Everybody sang "Happy Birthday" to me and I blew out all the candles. Then, I got six presents. After I opened my presents, everybody went home.

Setting: A birthday party at a house

Characters: Mary, Kimberly, Tanya, Amy, and a child having a birthday

Time: Summer

Events:
Beginning
1. There was a birthday party.
2. Four friends came to the party.
3. They played games and cards.
4. There was a chocolate birthday cake with white frosting and pink candles on top.
5. Everybody sang "Happy Birthday."
6. The child, whose birthday it was, blew out the candles.
7. There were six presents.
8. The presents were opened.
Ending
9. Everyone went home.

POLICE REPORT

DIRECTIONS: This activity is designed to help the students listen critically to a narration and determine which elements are present and which elements are missing. The students are then required to provide the missing information. Read the information about police reports to the students. Then read the police report in the box. Determine which story element is missing and answer the questions. Have the students draw a picture of the events.

When there has been an accident or a crime, the police need to send the information back to the police station. The police need to include all the necessary information so that their report can be understood easily.

Today there has been an accident. In the police report, some of the information is missing. Fill in the missing information and then use the police radio on the next page to relay the information back to the police station.

OFFICIAL POLICE REPORT

SETTING: Corner of Main and Park Streets

TIME: Monday afternoon about 4:00

EVENTS: The bicyclist was turning left onto Park Street. The dog ran out into the street, directly into the path of the bicyclist. The bicyclist swerved to avoid the dog. The bicyclist hit the curb and fell into a flower garden. The dog, bicycle, and bicycle rider were all unharmed. Some of the flowers appeared crushed.

The missing information is _____

_____

_____

Why is this information important? _____

_____

_____

SUGGESTED BOOKS

The following is a list of high-quality children's literature that may be used to facilitate narrative development. The first grouping of titles, listed below and on the following page, is arranged according to the skill emphasized. The second grouping, on page 44, contains additional titles of books that have been used with children to enhance narrative and story schema knowledge.

NARRATIVE ACT

NARRATOR
Himler, R. (1979). *Wake Up, Jeremiah.* New York: Harper & Row.
Noble, T.H. (1980). *The Day Jimmy's Boa Ate The Wash.* New York: Scholastic.
Schick, E. (1984). *A Piano for Julie.* New York: Greenwillow.
NARRATEE
Hughes, S. (1978). *David and Dog.* Englewood Cliffs, NJ: Prentice Hall.
Segal, L. (1970). *Tell Me a Mitzi.* New York: Farrar, Straus & Giroux.

NARRATIVE THEME (CONTENT)

PHYSICAL KNOWLEDGE
TIME CONCEPTS
Delton, J. (1974). *Two Good Friends.* New York: Crown.
George, J.C. (1972). *Julie of the Wolves.* New York: Harper & Row.
Grimm Brothers. (1972). *Snow White and the Seven Dwarfs.* New York: Farrar, Straus & Giroux.
Keats, E.J. (1962). *The Snowy Day.* New York: Viking.
L'Engle, M. (1962). *A Wrinkle in Time.* New York: Farrar, Straus & Giroux.
Pearce, P. (1958). *Tom's Midnight Garden.* Philadelphia: J.B. Lippincott.
CAUSALITY
Hall, D. (1979). *Ox-cart Man.* New York: Viking.
Hutchins, P. (1968). *Rosie's Walk.* New York: Viking.
Rylant, C. (1984). *This Year's Garden.* Scarsdale: Bradbury Press.

SOCIAL KNOWLEDGE

EMOTIONS
Care Bear Mini-Storybooks. New York: Random House.
Clifton, L. (1983). *Everett Anderson's Goodbye.* New York: Holt, Rinehart & Winston.
Keats, E.J. (1967). *Peter's Chair.* New York: Viking.
Oakley, G. (1981). *Hetty and Harriet.* New York: Atheneum.
Vigna. J. (1975). *Couldn't We Have A Turtle Instead?* Chicago: Albert Whitman.
Viorst, J. (1969). *I'll Fix Anthony.* New York: Harper & Row.
Wagner, J. (1977). *John Brown, Rose and the Midnight Cat.* Scarsdale: Bradbury Press.
TRICKERY
Leverich. K. (1978). *The Hungry Fox and the Foxy Duck.* New York: Parents Magazine.
Van Woerkman, D. (1977). *Harry and Shellbert.* New York. Macmillan.

Reprinted from *Topics in Language Disorders*, Vol. 7, No. 1, pp. 82-83, with permission of Aspen Publishers, Inc., © December 1986.

NARRATIVE STRUCTURE

MICROSTRUCTURE
Charlip, R. (1964). *Fortunately*. New York: Four Winds Press.
Griffith. H.V. (1980). *Mine Will, Said John*. New York: Greenwillow.

MACROSTRUCTURE
Bawden, N. (1985). *The Finding*. New York: Lothrop, Lee & Shepard.
Bruna. D. (1984). *A Story to Tell*. Los Angeles: Dick Bruna Books.
Cleary, B. (1981). *Ramona Quimby, Age 8*. New York: William Morrow.
Emberley, B. (1967). *Drummer Hoff*. Englewood Cliffs, NJ: Prentice Hall.
Goble, P. (1983). *Star Boy*. Scarsdale: Bradbury Press.
Graham, K. (1969). *The Wind in the Willows*. New York: Dell.
Kent, J. (1971). *The Fat Cat: A Danish Folktale*. New York: Scholastic.
McPhail, D. (1980). *Pig Pig Grows Up*. New York: E.P. Dutton.
Paterson, K. (1977). *Bridge to Terabithia*. New York: Thomas Y. Cromwell.
Sendak, M. (1963). *Where the Wild Things Are*. New York: Harper & Row.

Reprinted from *Topics in Language Disorders*, Vol. 7, No. 1, pp. 82-83, with permission of Aspen Publishers, Inc., © December 1986.

These additional books are also suggested:

Blume, J. (1985) *The Pain and The Great One*. New York: Dell.
Burch, R. (1980). *Ida Early Comes Over the Mountain*. New York: Viking Press.
Byars, B. (1987) *The Blossoms and the Green Phantom*. New York: Delacorte.
Byars, B. (1986) *The Blossoms Meet the Vulture Lady*. New York: Delacorte.
Byars, B. (1986) *The Not-Just-Anybody Family*. New York: Delacorte.
Cleary, B. (1983) *Dear Mr. Henshaw*. New York: Dell.
Curran, E. (1985) *Home For a Dinosaur*, Mahwah, NJ: Troll Associates.
Delton, J. (1974) *Two Good Friends*. New York: Crown.
Fleischman, S. (1986) *The Whipping Boy*. Mahwah, NJ: Troll Associates.
Greer, G. and Ruddick, B. (1987) *This Island Just Isn't Big Enough for the Four of Us*. New York: Harper and Row.
Hermes, P. (1986) *Kevin Corbett Eats Flies*. New York: Pocket Books.
Howe, D. and J. (1979) *Bunnicula*. New York: Atheneum Pub.
Howe, J. (1982) *Howliday Inn*. New York: Atheneum Pub.
Howe, J. (1983) *The Celery Stalks at Midnight*. New York: Atheneum Pub.
Howe, J. (1989) *Scared Silly: A Halloween Treat*. New York: Morrow Junior Books.
Mayer, M. (1983) *I Was So Mad*. New York: Golden Books.
Mayer, M. (1970) *A Special Trick*. New York: Dial Books for Young Readers.
Mayer, M. (1968) *There's A Nightmare in My Closet*. New York: Dial Books for Young Readers.
Nixon, J.L. (1986) *Beats Me, Claude*. New York: Viking.
Nixon, J.L. (1987) *If You Say So, Claude*. New York: Viking.
Prelutsky, J. (1983) *The Random House Book of Poetry for Children*. New York: Random House.
Steiner, B. (1986) *Oliver Dibbs and the Dinosaur Cause*. New York: Avon Books.
Viorst, J. (1974) *Rosie and Michael*. New York: Atheneum Pub.
Viorst, J. (1971) *The Tenth Good Thing About Barney*. New York: Atheneum Pub.

PRACTICE

The second aspect of *STORYBUILDING: A Guide to Structuring Oral Narratives* involves taking the knowledge of story elements and applying it to the production of narrations. Learning to narrate, as is learning most new skills, is a process. In the initial phase of developing narrative skills, the speech-language pathologist should provide a high degree of structure and facilitation. Gradually, this structure and facilitation can be reduced as the child acquires the needed skills.

Referring to the continuum (see page 14), note that added structure can be provided using:

1. Sequence picture cards
2. Story reformulation tasks
3. Story frames
4. Story starters

Facilitation can be provided by using scaffolding techniques. As previously stated, scaffolding involves the use of questioning techniques, by the facilitator, to organize story content (Page and Stewart, 1985). Westby (1985) defines scaffolds as "...temporary platforms or supports that are provided to learners that give them the guidance or information they need to build understanding and skills" (p. 184). The language disordered individual learns narration skills in contexts where a more skilled language user provides the framework necessary to complete the narrative. This framework is gradually faded as the child acquires these skills. Scaffolding questions to guide the speech-language pathologist are listed on page 47.

Applebee and Langer (1983) have devised a set of guidelines for judging the appropriateness of the scaffolding provided. Although these guidelines were developed as a means of evaluating instructional scaffolding used by teachers in particular school tasks, the principles also apply to scaffolding employed with language disordered individuals.

1. Intentionality: The narrative task has a clear, overall purpose. Any separate and additional activities contribute to the development of the child's narrative skills.
2. Appropriateness: The student is able to perform the narrative task with help, but would be unable to complete the task alone.
3. Structure: Modeling and questioning techniques lead to a natural sequence of thought and language.
4. Collaboration: Through modeling, rephrasing, and expansion, the speech-language pathologist responds to the student's attempts without rejecting what the child has produced.
5. Internalization: External scaffolding for the task is gradually reduced as the narrative structure is internalized by the student.

For more language-impaired students, the ability to produce a simple narrative may be the final goal in therapy. For other students, particularly adolescents, the goal may now be to produce a more complex narration. A narration increases in complexity by the inclusion of multiple character interactions and by embedded episodes, which will be addressed later in this section. As a word of caution, in this practice phase as well as in the critiquing phase, some vocabulary unfamiliar to the child may be present. For example, one story contains specialized football terms such as *end zone*. Students may also not be acquainted with story terms such as *episodes, secondary characters*, etc. The speech-language pathologist may wish to modify these terms or provide a brief training exercise to teach these terms.

Activities that provide structure are presented in the next sections. Each section begins with an explanation, directions on how to complete the tasks, and an example. Suggested, sample IEP goals are also provided for each of the sections. These activities are organized into six sections:

1. Sequence picture cards
2. Story reformulation tasks
3. Story frames
4. Story starters
5. Multiple character interactions
6. Embedded episodes

SCAFFOLDING QUESTIONS

SETTING OF THE STORY

Where does the story take place?

CHARACTERS OF THE STORY

Who are the main characters?

TIME OF THE STORY

When does the story take place?

EVENTS OF THE STORY

What happens to the characters?

GOAL(S) OF THE CHARACTERS

What are the characters trying to do?

PLAN(S) OF THE CHARACTERS

How will the characters reach their goal?

ATTEMPTS

What happens when the characters try to reach their goal?

RESULTS

How does everything turn out?

ENDING

How does the story end?

SEQUENCE PICTURE CARDS

The use of sequence picture cards is one method of providing additional structure in the development of narrative skills. Sequence picture cards are ideal for individuals who have difficulty ordering events temporally. These cards supply some of the content while the student must provide the structure. However, sequence cards do have limitations. Language and learning disabled students will often only describe the content of the pictures rather than linking the events and recognizing cause and effect relationships.

DIRECTIONS: Begin with two pictures of a simple action sequence. Ask the child to tell a story about what is happening in the pictures. Fill out the narrative form on page 50, emphasizing the narrative elements (e.g., "Right, there is a boy and his mother in the picture. They are the characters in our story"). Gradually increase the number of sequence cards. Clinician modeling and scaffolding techniques may be used when the child has difficulty narrating the sequence. After the narrative form has been completed, ask the child to retell the story using the form as a guide. These narratives can then be told to a partner, tape recorder, transcriber, or written as a story. These narratives can also be sent home for further practice. An example *Narration Elements* form is on the next page.

SAMPLE I.E.P. GOAL

The student will be able to produce a complete narrative, containing the story elements of setting, characters, time, beginning event, and ending event, using picture sequence cards, with 90% or greater accuracy.

NARRATION ELEMENTS

Name: _____ Date: _____

Description of Sequence Cards: _6 cards; A boy riding his bike, falls,_
gets hurt. Mom puts on a bandage.

SETTING

Outdoors

CHARACTERS

A little boy, his mom

TIME

Daytime

EVENTS

Beginning
1. A little boy is riding his bike.
2. There was a log in the way. He hit the log.
3. The bike tipped over and the little boy fell off.
4. He had a sore knee. He was crying.
5. He ran home.

Ending
6. His mom put a bandage on his sore knee.

Using this form, retell the story.

NARRATION ELEMENTS

Name: _____ Date: _____

Description of Sequence Cards: _____

_____

SETTING

CHARACTERS

TIME

EVENTS

   Beginning

   Ending

Using this form, retell the story.

STORY REFORMULATION

Reformulating stories is another method of practicing narrative skills. In a story reformulation task, the story content and structure are provided. The child is then required to reformulate the content and structure in a logical, appropriate way. Because of memory limitations, the child would not be expected to repeat the story verbatim. Rather, the story elements of setting, characters, time, and the sequence of events should be retained. Interestingly, children who are not producing cause and effect statements, multiple character interactions, and embedded episodes in their own narratives will often be able to retell a story containing these more advanced linguistic components.

DIRECTIONS: Read the story to the child. Ask the child if he/she could understand the story. Explain anything that is not clear. Instruct the child to retell the story and write or tape-record the child's response. Then, with the child, answer the questions at the bottom of the page pertaining to the child's reformulated story.

SAMPLE I.E.P. GOAL

The student will be able to reformulate a story, containing the story elements of setting, characters, time, beginning and ending events, with 90% or greater accuracy.

STORY REFORMULATION 1

Tom's grandmother gave him a pretty, green plant for his bedroom. She told him the plant needed water and sunlight. Tom forgot to water the plant. In a few days, it had wilted and died.

Retell this story.

> Tom's grandmother gave him a plant. His grandmother told him to water the plant and give it good sunlight. He forgot to water the plant. Then it got all yukky.

Looking at the student's story:

Is there a setting?	Yes	(No)
Are the characters given?	(Yes)	No
Is the time given?	Yes	(No)
Are the events given in order?	(Yes)	No
Does the story make sense?	Yes	(No)
Could someone else understand this story?	Yes	(No)
Is all the necessary information presented?	Yes	(No)

If there are any *No* responses, then retell the story.

STORY REFORMULATION 1

Tom's grandmother gave him a pretty, green plant for his bedroom. She told him the plant needed water and sunlight. Tom forgot to water the plant. In a few days, it had wilted and died.

_____

Retell this story.

_____

Looking at the student's story:

Is there a setting?	Yes	No
Are the characters given?	Yes	No
Is the time given?	Yes	No
Are the events given in order?	Yes	No
Does the story make sense?	Yes	No
Could someone else understand this story?	Yes	No
Is all the necessary information presented?	Yes	No

If there are any _No_ responses, then retell the story.

STORY REFORMULATION 2

There was a football game last Friday night. The teams were tied. The quarterback threw the ball to David. It was too high. David jumped as high as he could. He caught the ball and ran into the end zone. His team won the game.

_____

Retell this story.

_____

Looking at the student's story:

Is there a setting?	Yes	No
Are the characters given?	Yes	No
Is the time given?	Yes	No
Are the events given in order?	Yes	No
Does the story make sense?	Yes	No
Could someone else understand this story?	Yes	No
Is all the necessary information presented?	Yes	No

If there are any *No* responses, then retell the story.

STORY REFORMULATION 3

Dacia wanted to buy a Nintendo® game but she didn't have enough money. Her parents said they would pay her for doing extra chores at home. After school and on weekends, she helped her mom and dad. Soon, Dacia had earned enough money to buy the Nintendo® game. After she bought the Nintendo®, she invited her friends to come over and play.

_____

Retell this story.

_____

Looking at the student's story:

Is there a setting?	Yes	No
Are the characters given?	Yes	No
Is the time given?	Yes	No
Are the events given in order?	Yes	No
Does the story make sense?	Yes	No
Could someone else understand this story?	Yes	No
Is all the necessary information presented?	Yes	No

If there are any *No* responses, then retell the story.

STORY REFORMULATION 4

Jeremy had to study for his math test the next day. He didn't watch TV after school. He didn't play ball with his friends. He didn't read comic books. He studied all night until 9:00. The next day, Jeremy took the math test. When the teacher handed back the tests, Jeremy had an A.

Retell this story.

Looking at the student's story:

Is there a setting?	Yes	No
Are the characters given?	Yes	No
Is the time given?	Yes	No
Are the events given in order?	Yes	No
Does the story make sense?	Yes	No
Could someone else understand this story?	Yes	No
Is all the necessary information presented?	Yes	No

If there are any *No* responses, then retell the story.

STORY REFORMULATION 5

It was the Fourth of July. Bianca's aunt told her to be careful because the sparklers were very hot. Bianca wanted to see if the sparklers were really hot. She touched the end of the sparkler with her finger. It was very hot. Bianca had a blister on her finger.

Retell this story.

Looking at the student's story:

Is there a setting?	Yes	No
Are the characters given?	Yes	No
Is the time given?	Yes	No
Are the events given in order?	Yes	No
Does the story make sense?	Yes	No
Could someone else understand this story?	Yes	No
Is all the necessary information presented?	Yes	No

If there are any *No* responses, then retell the story.

STORY FRAME

The use of a story frame is another way of providing additional structure in the development of narrative skills. A story frame has been defined as a series of spaces linked together by key narrative elements that reflect a specific line of thought (Fowler, 1982). This framework allows the student to focus on the content of the story, since the structure has been provided. Using the framework forces the student to maintain the topic, order events sequentially, consider the perspective(s) of the characters, and recognize cause and effect relationships and outcomes.

DIRECTIONS: This activity can be done in a large or small group as well as individually. Using one of the topics given or one selected by the students, ask the children to recall something that has occurred in the past or make up a story about that topic. As the child tells the story, the clinician fills in the appropriate blanks on the story frame. (See the example on the next page.) After the story frame has been completed, the child will then retell the story using the filled-in story frame as a guide. Point out to the students how the use of connecting terms such as "first...," "next...," and "In the end..." help the speaker and the listener organize the narrative. Six story frame topics have been included. An additional page has been provided that will accommodate any story frame topics.

SAMPLE I.E.P. GOAL

The student will be able to produce, with 90% or greater accuracy, a complete narrative, containing the story elements of setting, characters, time, goal, plan, events, and results, when using a story frame.

STORY FRAME

This story took place at _a store._

The time was _a couple of years ago._ The characters
in the story were _me, my sister, my dad, and a lady who worked at_
the store.

The first event was _my sister and I were at this store with my dad._
We went into the bathroom. My sister accidentally knocked the roll
of toilet paper into the toilet.

The characters felt _embarrassed and a little nervous, because we_
didn't want to get in trouble.

The goal was _to get the toilet paper out of the toilet._

The plan to reach the goal was _first, we tried to reach it but we didn't_
want to stick our fingers in there. So we flushed the toilet. We
thought we could flush it down.

The next events were _the roll got stuck and the toilet started to back_
up. We thought it would overflow. A lady who worked at the store
came in the bathroom so we ran over by our dad. He was looking at
tires.

The results were _we told Dad we wanted to go home. Dad said,_
"Okay." So we left.

In the end the characters felt _scared still. Whenever Dad goes to that_
store, we wait for him in the car.

STORYBUILDING

AFTER SCHOOL

This story took place at _____ .

The time was _____ .

The characters in the story were _____

_____ .

The first event was _____

_____

_____ .

The characters felt _____

_____ .

The goal was _____

_____ .

The plan to reach the goal was _____

_____

_____ .

The next events were _____

_____

_____ .

The results were _____

_____

_____ .

In the end the characters felt _____

_____ .

ON HALLOWEEN

This story took place at _____ .

The time was _____ .

The characters in the story were _____

_____ .

The first event was _____

_____

_____ .

The characters felt _____

_____ .

The goal was _____

_____ .

The plan to reach the goal was _____

_____

_____ .

The next events were _____

_____

_____

_____ .

The results were _____

_____

_____ .

In the end the characters felt _____

_____ .

STORYBUILDING

IN THE SUMMER

This story took place at _____ .

The time was _____ .

The characters in the story were _____

_____ .

The first event was _____

_____

_____ .

The characters felt _____

_____ .

The goal was _____

_____ .

The plan to reach the goal was _____

_____

_____ .

The next events were _____

_____

_____

_____ .

The results were _____

_____

_____ .

In the end the characters felt _____

_____ .

STORYBUILDING

AT THE PEP RALLY

RAH-RAH!
Go Team, Go!

This story took place at _____.

The time was _____.

The characters in the story were _____

_____.

The first event was _____

_____

_____.

The characters felt _____

_____.

The goal was _____

_____.

The plan to reach the goal was _____

_____

_____.

The next events were _____

_____

_____

_____.

The results were _____

_____

_____.

In the end the characters felt _____

_____.

STORYBUILDING

IN MY ROOM

This story took place at _____ .

The time was _____ .

The characters in the story were _____

_____ .

The first event was _____

_____

_____ .

The characters felt _____

_____ .

The goal was _____

_____ .

The plan to reach the goal was _____

_____

_____ .

The next events were _____

_____

_____ .

The results were _____

_____

_____ .

In the end the characters felt _____

_____ .

IN MATH CLASS

This story took place at _____ .

The time was _____ .

The characters in the story were _____

_____ .

The first event was _____

_____

_____ .

The characters felt _____

_____ .

The goal was _____

_____ .

The plan to reach the goal was _____

_____

_____ .

The next events were _____

_____

_____ .

The results were _____

_____

_____ .

In the end the characters felt _____

_____ .

STORY FRAME

This story took place at _____ .

The time was _____ . The characters

in the story were _____

_____ .

The first event was _____

_____

_____ .

The characters felt _____

_____ .

The goal was _____

_____ .

The plan to reach the goal was _____

_____

_____ .

The next events were _____

_____

_____

_____ .

The results were _____

_____

_____ .

In the end the characters felt _____

_____ .

STORYBUILDING

STORY STARTERS

The use of story starters is another method of providing additional structure. Story starters are sentences which may contain setting, characters, time, and an initiating event. The student is then required to complete the story in a logical manner consistent with the information already presented. Story starters are particularly beneficial for students who often include irrelevant or extraneous information in their stories.

DIRECTIONS: In a large or small group, select the first story starter. Identify the story elements given (e.g., characters, setting, goal, beginning event, etc.). Brainstorm further events and outcomes. Remind the students that all their sentences must be related to the story starter. The next step is for the students to create their own narratives using the story starter. These narratives can then be told to a partner, tape recorder, transcriber, or put in written form. Six story starter pages have been provided with a simpler version used for story starters one to three and a more complex version used for story starters four to six. Two additional pages, with one of each of these forms, have been provided so that any story starter sentences may be used.

SAMPLE I.E.P. GOALS

1. The student will be able to produce, with 90% or greater accuracy, a complete narrative containing the story elements of setting, characters, time, beginning and ending events, when using a story starter.

2. The student will be able to produce, with 90% or greater accuracy, a complete narrative containing the story elements of setting, characters, time, goal, plan, events, and results, when using a story starter.

STORY STARTER 1

One day, I was walking home from school with my brother and a dinosaur followed us home.

SETTING: *Walking home from school*

CHARACTERS: *Me, my brother, a dinosaur*

TIME: *After school*

BEGINNING EVENT: *I was walking home from school with my brother and a dinosaur followed us home.*

SECOND EVENT: *We recognized the dinosaur. He was from the museum. He must have run away and gotten lost.*

NEXT EVENTS: *We decided to take the dinosaur back to the museum. So we walked towards the museum and the dinosaur followed us. The big doors at the museum were still open. So we walked inside the museum and the dinosaur followed us.*

RESULTS: *There was no one around so we hurried to get the dinosaur back to the right place in the museum.*

ENDING: *We said good-bye to the dinosaur, and then we ran out of the museum and all the way home. We told Mom we were late because a dinosaur followed us home but she didn't believe us.*

STORY STARTER 1

One day, I was walking home from school with my brother and a dinosaur followed us home.

SETTING: _____

_____

CHARACTERS: _____

_____

TIME: _____

_____

BEGINNING EVENT: _____

_____

SECOND EVENT: _____

_____

NEXT EVENTS: _____

_____

_____

_____

RESULTS: _____

_____

ENDING: _____

_____

_____

STORY STARTER 2

My friend Pat and I ate hot lunch at school Friday, and it made us invisible.

SETTING: _____

_____

CHARACTERS: _____

_____

TIME: _____

_____

BEGINNING EVENT: _____

_____

SECOND EVENT: _____

_____

NEXT EVENTS: _____

_____

_____

_____

RESULTS: _____

_____

ENDING: _____

_____

_____

STORY STARTER 3

When the principal of our school went home sick, I became principal for the day.

SETTING: _____

_____

CHARACTERS: _____

_____

TIME: _____

_____

BEGINNING EVENT: _____

_____

SECOND EVENT: _____

_____

NEXT EVENTS: _____

_____

_____

_____

_____

RESULTS: _____

_____

ENDING: _____

_____

_____

STORY STARTER 4

Paul knew he had invented something that had never been invented before.

SETTING: _____

_____

CHARACTERS: _____

_____

TIME: _____

_____

BEGINNING EVENT: _____

_____

NEXT EVENT: _____

_____

GOAL: _____

_____

PLAN: _____

_____

_____

_____

NEXT EVENTS: _____

_____

_____

_____

RESULTS: _____

_____

ENDING: _____

_____

_____

STORY STARTER 5

I was home alone in the kitchen, when suddenly I heard footsteps coming down the stairs towards me.

SETTING: _____

_____

CHARACTERS: _____

_____

TIME: _____

_____

BEGINNING EVENT: _____

_____

NEXT EVENT: _____

_____

GOAL: _____

_____

PLAN: _____

_____

_____

NEXT EVENTS: _____

_____

_____

_____

RESULTS: _____

_____

ENDING: _____

_____

_____

STORY STARTER 6

As soon as I put my hand in the pocket, I knew that I had taken the wrong coat.

SETTING: _____

_____

CHARACTERS: _____

_____

TIME: _____

_____

BEGINNING EVENT: _____

_____

NEXT EVENT: _____

_____

GOAL: _____

_____

PLAN: _____

_____

_____

_____

NEXT EVENTS: _____

_____

_____

_____

_____

RESULTS: _____

_____

ENDING: _____

_____

_____

STORYBUILDING

STORY STARTER

SETTING: _____

_____

CHARACTERS: _____

_____

TIME: _____

_____

BEGINNING EVENT: _____

_____

SECOND EVENT: _____

_____

NEXT EVENTS: _____

_____

_____

_____

_____

RESULTS: _____

_____

ENDING: _____

_____

_____

STORY STARTER

SETTING: _____

_____

CHARACTERS: _____

_____

TIME: _____

_____

BEGINNING EVENT: _____

_____

NEXT EVENT: _____

_____

GOAL: _____

_____

PLAN: _____

_____

_____

_____

NEXT EVENTS: _____

_____

_____

_____

_____

RESULTS: _____

_____

ENDING: _____

_____

_____

MULTIPLE CHARACTER INTERACTIONS

Multiple character interaction refers to stories with more than one character. These characters may have separate goals and plans but their actions influence the other(s). By the age of 7-8 years, most normally developing children are capable of understanding stories with multiple character interactions (Gmeiner Heinrich, 1989). By the age of 11-12, children are capable of producing a story which contains multiple character interactions (Gmeiner Heinrich, 1989). An example of a story, from children's literature, with multiple character interactions would be *Snow White*. In this example, the actions of Snow White and the Wicked Queen affect each other.

Language and learning disabled children often do not recognize that different characters in stories have differing goals and emotions. In the production of narratives, these same children may not identify characters appropriately, or be able to assume the characters' perspectives.

On page 80, a form has been included that will help the student to construct a narration with multiple character interactions. No story topics have been given so that this page may be reproduced. An example of a story with multiple character interactions has been provided.

DIRECTIONS: This activity can be done in a large or small group as well as individually. With discussions and role-playing help, the students become aware that characters in stories may have different goals, plans, and actions that influence the other characters. Some of the suggested books from the *Familiarization* section may be helpful. Instruct the child to make up a story or recall an event from the past in which one character's actions affected another character. As the student tells the story, fill in the appropriate spaces using the form on page 80. Help the student to complete all of the spaces. Have the child retell the story using the completed form. This story should be tape-recorded. As the taped story is played back, answer the questions on the bottom of the page.

SAMPLE I.E.P. GOAL

The student will be able to produce, with 90% or greater accuracy, a complete narrative, containing setting, multiple character interactions, time, goal, plan, and beginning and ending events.

SAMPLE STORY WITH MULTIPLE CHARACTER INTERACTION

Once there was a man who lived alone in the forest. He didn't want to live around other people. He was a gentle man who was trusted by the animals of the forest. During the spring, summer, and fall seasons, the man would collect berries, catch fish, and grow food. He would store the food for the long, cold winter.

One day the man went out in the woods to find some blueberries. He walked a long way to find the berries. When he returned to his cabin, everything was a mess. Jars, cans, and sacks of food were tipped over and spilled on the floor. There were fruits and vegetables everywhere. The man did not know who could have done this. There were no other people around and the animals never went inside his cabin. The man cleaned up his cabin and then went outside. As he stepped out of the cabin, he realized that the forest was silent. No birds were singing and no squirrels scurried by. The man knew immediately that something was wrong.

On a hill overlooking the cabin sat a hungry watchful fox. He saw the man go back into the cabin. The fox slowly made his way down the hill towards the cabin.

Inside the cabin, the man took out an old rifle. It was covered with dust. Carefully, the man dusted off the rifle and began to load it with shells. At that moment, the vicious fox stalked angrily outside the cabin. The man slowly opened the cabin door and stepped outside. He saw the fox. The man quickly raised his rifle, pointed it at the tallest tree, and fired. The noise frightened the fox, who turned and ran back up the hill to watch the man. The man stood there a long time and finally went inside the cabin. The man was afraid. He knew that he had frightened off the fox for now, but he also knew that the fox would return soon.

MULTIPLE CHARACTER INTERACTIONS

MAIN CHARACTER 1 _A man_   MAIN CHARACTER 2 _A fox_

SETTING _a forest_   SETTING _a forest_

TIME _one day_   TIME _one day_

GOAL _To get rid of the fox_   GOAL _To find some food_

PLAN _To fire his gun and frighten away the fox_   PLAN _To attack the man and steal his food_

EVENTS _1.) The man went looking for berries._   EVENTS _1.) The fox went into the man's cabin looking for food._

2.) When he returned, the man found fruits and vegetables on the floor of his cabin.   _2.) The fox watched the man return._

     3.) The fox stood outside the cabin.

3.) The man cleaned and loaded his old gun and fired it into the trees.   _4.) The loud noise frightened the fox._

ENDING _The man was frightened because he knew the fox would return._   ENDING _The hungry fox ran away to the hill to watch the man._

Discussion Questions

1. Were the goals for characters 1 and 2 the same or different?
   different   The man's goal was to get rid of the fox.
   The fox's goal was to find food.

2. Were the plans for characters 1 and 2 the same or different?
   different   The man's plan was to frighten the fox with the gun.
   The fox's plan was to attack the man and steal his food.

3. Did any of the events of character 1 affect character 2? How?
   Yes   The man's firing the gun caused the fox to run away.

4. Did any of the events of character 2 affect character 1? How?
   Yes   The man took out his gun after the fox had made a mess of the cabin.

5. Was there anything that one character did that made another character do, feel, or say something? What?
   Yes   The man saw the fox run up the hill and he felt afraid, because he knew the fox would return.

MULTIPLE CHARACTER INTERACTIONS

MAIN CHARACTER 1 _____   MAIN CHARACTER 2 _____

SETTING _____   SETTING _____

TIME _____   TIME _____

GOAL _____   GOAL _____

PLAN _____   PLAN _____

_____   _____

EVENTS _____   EVENTS _____

_____   _____

_____   _____

_____   _____

_____   _____

_____   _____

_____   _____

_____   _____

_____   _____

ENDING _____   ENDING _____

_____   _____

Discussion Questions

1. Were the goals for characters 1 and 2 the same or different?

2. Were the plans for characters 1 and 2 the same or different?

3. Did any of the events of character 1 affect character 2? How?

4. Did any of the events of character 2 affect character 1? How?

5. Was there anything that one character did that made another character do, feel, or say something? What?

EMBEDDED EPISODES

A competent storyteller is able to arrange the flow of information to ensure the listener's understanding (Johnston, 1982). In conversational speech, a skilled communicator has many verbal devices at hand to accomplish this understanding. The speaker may rely on asides, flashbacks, introductions, and background information all embedded within the context of a narration. The speaker then needs to juggle multiple settings, characters, times, and events in a logical and appropriate way.

Although it is not clear when children acquire these conversational tools, certainly most middle and high school students are capable of understanding and using embedded episodes. Often the retelling of a movie, book, or TV program plot requires the speaker to be proficient at handling multiple and intertwined episodes.

On page 84, a form has been included to help the students structure narratives with embedded episodes. No story topics have been given so that this page may be reproduced. An example of a story with an embedded episode has also been provided.

DIRECTIONS: This activity can be accomplished in a large or small group as well as individually. Discuss with the students why a story might contain embedded episodes. Again, the suggested books from the *Familiarization* section may be used. Help the child to construct a story using the form on page 84. Have the child retell the story using the completed form. This story should be tape-recorded. As the taped story is played back, answer the questions on the bottom of the page.

SAMPLE I.E.P. GOAL

The student will be able to produce, with 90% or greater accuracy, a complete narrative with embedded episodes. Each episode will contain setting, characters, time, and beginning and ending events.

SAMPLE STORY WITH AN EMBEDDED EPISODE

One time last summer, I went swimming in Lake Wissota with my friend MaryAnne. We were swimming off the dock at my house. Actually, I was swimming and MaryAnne was sitting on the dock. MaryAnne hasn't gone swimming since she was about six years old. When she was six, she was swimming and she swam to a real deep part, over her head. She couldn't swim back to the shore. She was really afraid. She kept going under the water. Finally, her brother saw her and saved her. So since then, MaryAnne doesn't like to swim.

Anyway, on this day, I was swimming and I found something in the sand on the bottom of the lake. It was a box, buried in the sand. I wanted to open the box and see what was inside. I kept diving down to the bottom and pushing the sand away but I couldn't lift the box. It was buried too deep in the sand. I called MaryAnne to come and help me. She didn't want to go in the water but I talked her into it. Together, we kept pulling on the box. We tried for a long time but we couldn't move the box. We were so tired we had to stop. All that night, we tried to imagine what was in the box. The next day, we went back down to the lake to look for the box. Of course, MaryAnne didn't want to go in the water so I went by myself. I looked everywhere but I couldn't find the box. I thought I knew where the box was buried but I couldn't find it. MaryAnne even came in the lake to look for the box. We looked for two days but we never found the box again. Maybe the box got covered by sand again or we forgot where it was. We are going to look again, next summer, for that box.

EMBEDDED EPISODES

EPISODE 1 (Primary)

Setting ___Lake Wissota___

Characters ___The narrator, Mary Anne___

Time ___Last summer___

Events

Beginning ___1.) The narrator went swimming in Lake Wissota. 2.) Mary Anne sat on the dock. 3.) There was a box buried in the sand. 4.) The box was stuck. 5.) Mary Anne went in the lake and together they tried to free the box. 6.) They stopped because they were tired and imagined what was in the box. 7.) When they returned the next day, they couldn't find the box.___

Ending ___8.) They are going to look for the box next summer.___

EPISODE 2 (Secondary)

Setting ___Not given___

Characters ___Mary Anne, Mary Anne's brother___

Time ___When Mary Anne was 6___

Events

Beginning ___1.) Mary Anne was swimming. 2.) She swam to a deep part which was over her head. 3.) She couldn't swim back to shore. 4.) She was afraid and kept going under. 5.) Her brother saw her and saved her.___

Ending ___6.) Since that time, Mary Anne doesn't like to swim.___

Discussion Questions

1. A secondary or embedded episode is included in a story to give more information or to explain something further. Why was an embedded episode included in this story? _The secondary episode was a flashback to an earlier incident that explained a character's fear of swimming._

2. The secondary episode must be related to the primary episode (e. g., the same characters, the same setting, etc.). How are these two episodes related? _Mary Anne is a main character in both episodes and both episodes are about swimming._

3. When telling a story, we should <u>not</u> jump from one episode to the other. Why do you think this is true? _It would be too confusing to the listener._

4. As a rule, we should begin with the primary episode, give the entire secondary episode, and finish with the primary episode. Why do you think this would be best? _So the story will be clear and easy to understand._

5. Tell the story in a way that would be confusing to the listener.

6. Now, tell this story in a way that would be clear to the listener.

EMBEDDED EPISODES

EPISODE 1 (Primary)	EPISODE 2 (Secondary)

Setting _____

_____

Characters _____

_____

Time _____

Events

Beginning _____

_____

_____

_____

_____

_____

_____

_____

_____

Ending _____

_____

Setting _____

_____

Characters _____

_____

Time _____

Events

Beginning _____

_____

_____

_____

_____

_____

_____

_____

_____

Ending _____

_____

Discussion Questions

1. A secondary or embedded episode is included in a story to give more information or to explain something further. Why was an embedded episode included in this story?

2. The secondary episode must be related to the primary episode (e. g., the same characters, the same setting, etc.). How are these two episodes related?

3. When telling a story, we should <u>not</u> jump from one episode to the other. Why do you think this is true?

4. As a rule, we should begin with the primary episode, give the entire secondary episode, and finish with the primary episode. Why do you think this would be best?

5. Tell the story in a way that would be confusing to the listener.

6. Now, tell this story in a way that would be clear to the listener.

CRITIQUING

While the students are developing and expanding their narrative skills, they also need to include the third aspect of the *STORYBUILDING* program: *Critiquing*. This third phase involves the critiquing and discussing of oral narratives. Suggested, sample IEP goals have been provided on page 86. Critiquing narratives reinforces the students' knowledge of story elements and allows the students to view a narration as a whole. Narratives function as a means of communicating and conveying information. The students must now determine whether the narratives presented serve that function.

Included in this section are 20 narratives produced by language delayed/disordered children and normally developing children. In some of these narratives, slight changes have been made for purposes of clarification. Idiomatic expressions were intentionally left in the narrative samples to be more representative of children's language. Grammatical errors were also left in to illustrate the connection between these errors and lack of clarity. The speech-language pathologist may wish to modify these narratives and collect more narrative samples from language-impaired as well as normally developing children.

To aid in the selection of narratives for critiquing, a list of the narratives produced by language-impaired students and normally developing children has been given. The narrations produced by normally developing children have been numbered 1, 2, 3, 6, 8, 11, 14, 15, 16, 17, 18, 19, 20. The narrations produced by language-impaired students have been numbered 4, 5, 7, 9, 10, 12, 13. Instruct the child that now it is his/her turn to be the teacher or clinician. Tell the child to listen to the story as it is read and then judge whether or not it was a good story (i.e., it was easy to understand and the story made sense). Using the basic narrative form, provided below the story or on the following page, determine which elements are present and which are missing, and how this affected the listener's ability to understand the story. At the end of this section, critiques for these narratives have been provided. Since the *Narration Elements* form will accommodate any type of narrative, this form has been used for all 20 critiques of the narrative samples. The *Story Grammar Elements* form (see page 38 of the *Familiarization* section) has also been used for the last five narrative samples. These critiques are intended merely as a guide for critiquing, since actual wording will vary.

Ultimately, the goal of this program is for the child to self-monitor and self-correct his/her own narratives. Therefore, the critiquing phase also requires the child to analyze his/her own narratives. Ask the child to tell a story about any topic. This story should then be tape-recorded. The listener or listeners should give immediate feedback to the speaker regarding the strengths and weaknesses of the narrative. Some example comments might be:

I liked the way you told us who the people are. It really made sense when you explained it that way.

When you told us that it happened one night when you were home alone, right away we were interested and wanted to hear the rest of the story.

You told us that this was a movie you saw. When you said, "This one big guy chased the guy," I was confused. I didn't understand who the people were and why one person chased another.

Some of the questions that could be asked of the speaker would be:

Did you tell the story the way you wanted to?

Do you think the listeners could follow the story as you told it?

If you heard somebody tell this story, could you understand it?

Did you remember to include the characters, setting, time, and the events in the right order?

After the speaker has heard the listeners' comments and discussed his/her own perceptions, play back the tape recording. Discuss with the child the strengths and weaknesses cited by the listeners. Help the child to determine ways to improve the narrative.

SAMPLE I.E.P. GOALS

1. A. The student will state, with 90% or greater accuracy, which key components of a given narration are present and which are missing when critiquing narratives.

   B. Using this critique, the student will then judge, with 90% or greater accuracy, whether this narration was clear and easy to understand.

2. The student will correctly state, with 90% or greater accuracy, whether his/her own narrative was clear and easy to understand, following a tape recording of that narrative.

NARRATION 1

Name: _____

Date: _____

Tomorrow, I am going to make Rice Krispies® bars by myself. It's very easy to make them. First, you melt some butter. Then you put in the marshmallows and melt them too. You have to stir them so they don't stick. After the marshmallows are smooth and melted then you measure the Rice Krispies® and put them in the pan with the marshmallows. You have to mix it all up very well. Then you put the Rice Krispies® stuff in one of those long cake pans. You have to spread out the Rice Krispies® in the pan. Then you put the pan in the refrigerator. When the Rice Krispies® get hard, then your mom cuts them and you eat them.

NARRATION ELEMENTS

SETTING

CHARACTERS

TIME

EVENTS

  Beginning

  Ending

Was this story clear and easy to understand? _____
Why? _____

_____

_____

If the story was not clear, what could we do to make the story clearer and easier to understand? _____

_____

_____

NARRATION 2

Name: _____

Date: _____

Once my mom and dad and I were going to my grandma's house. It was on Thanksgiving and this big deer ran out in front of our car. My dad stopped the car. The deer ran across the road and into the woods. We waited there for about a minute. Then two more deer ran across the road. My dad said there are always lots of deer on that road.

NARRATION ELEMENTS

SETTING

CHARACTERS

TIME

EVENTS

Beginning

Ending

Was this story clear and easy to understand? _____

Why? _____

_____

_____

If the story was not clear, what could we do to make the story clearer and easier to understand? _____

_____

_____

NARRATION 3

Name: _____

Date: _____

One time I went camping in Minnesota with my family. Our dog Peanut came too. My mom got up in the night to close the windows. It was starting to rain. When she looked in her bed, Peanut was sleeping in my mom's sleeping bag.

NARRATION ELEMENTS

SETTING

CHARACTERS

TIME

EVENTS

   Beginning

   Ending

Was this story clear and easy to understand? _____

Why? _____

_____

_____

If the story was not clear, what could we do to make the story clearer and easier to understand? _____

_____

_____

NARRATION 4

Name: _____

Date: _____

On the days that there are basketball games, there are pep rallies. The cheerleaders go to all the grades. It's in the gym. The kids cheer. One class gets this stick thing. The coach talks sometimes. That's all.

NARRATION ELEMENTS

SETTING

CHARACTERS

TIME

EVENTS

   Beginning

   Ending

Was this story clear and easy to understand? _____

Why? _____

_____

If the story was not clear, what could we do to make the story clearer and easier to understand? _____

_____

_____

NARRATION 5

I saw this one show on TV. These guys were fighting and there was one bomb. The bomb blew up the girl's car. The police came and one guy ran away. The police chased him. The guy jumped in the water and started to swim away. The police jumped in the water too. The police catched him.

NARRATION ELEMENTS

SETTING

CHARACTERS

TIME

EVENTS

  Beginning

  Ending

Was this story clear and easy to understand? _____

Why? _____

_____

_____

If the story was not clear, what could we do to make the story clearer and easier to understand? _____

_____

_____

NARRATION 6

Name: _____

Date: _____

I saw this movie on TV. It had these monsters in it. One monster was really tall and green and everyone was afraid of him. Then, this little girl got lost and everyone was afraid the monster would kill her. They all went looking for this girl. They couldn't find her so they went to where the monster lived. The monster had the little girl. The people were crying and the little girl was crying too. She liked the monster and wanted to stay with him. But she had to go home. She gave her doll to the monster and then no one was afraid of the monster. He was nice.

NARRATION ELEMENTS

SETTING

CHARACTERS

TIME

EVENTS

  Beginning

  Ending

Was this story clear and easy to understand? _____
Why? _____
_____
_____

If the story was not clear, what could we do to make the story clearer and easier to understand? _____
_____
_____

NARRATION 7

Name: _____

Date: _____

My mom and dad got divorced, and when I go to my dad's house then we get to go to Jellystone. And we get to go swimming, play golfing and we get to eat some nachos. And we get to play this one game where you shoot the other guy before they shoot you and sometimes we shoot pool. Sometimes, we buy stuff and sometimes we have to go to our mom's. Sometimes, we don't get to go to our dad's house for a long time because our mom keeps us here 'cause we have to go to school.

_____

NARRATION ELEMENTS

SETTING

CHARACTERS

TIME

EVENTS

  Beginning

  Ending

Was this story clear and easy to understand? _____

Why? _____

_____

_____

If the story was not clear, what could we do to make the story clearer and easier to understand? _____

_____

_____

NARRATION 8

Name: _____

Date: _____

My dad and I went fishing in Canada this summer, on a big lake. It's 90 square miles. There are many bays and many rivers attached to it. I caught a lot of fish and probably the highlight of my trip was catching a 42 inch, 17 pound northern. It cost too much to get the whole thing done but I did get the head mounted. It's on a plaque in my room. I guess we're going back next year.

_____

NARRATION ELEMENTS

SETTING

CHARACTERS

TIME

EVENTS

   Beginning

   Ending

Was this story clear and easy to understand? _____

Why? _____

_____

_____

If the story was not clear, what could we do to make the story clearer and easier to understand? _____

_____

_____

NARRATION 9

Name: _____

Date: _____

I have this collection. Well, I have lots of collections. I collect lots of things. I keep things. I collect little cars and I collect seashells. From the ocean. Have you ever seen the ocean? They have lots of shells. I know many things about the ocean.

_____

NARRATION ELEMENTS

SETTING

CHARACTERS

TIME

EVENTS

   Beginning

   Ending

Was this story clear and easy to understand? _____
Why? _____

_____

_____

If the story was not clear, what could we do to make the story clearer and easier to understand? _____

_____

_____

NARRATION 10

Name: _____

Date: _____

One day in the summertime, I was at the pool. The new pool. And you know Marvin? He's in another grade. He pushed me in the water. The lady that watches the pool, the...what's her name? The lifeguard. The lifeguard never saw him. So I pushed him in the water.

NARRATION ELEMENTS

SETTING

CHARACTERS

TIME

EVENTS

Beginning

Ending

Was this story clear and easy to understand? _____

Why? _____

_____

_____

If the story was not clear, what could we do to make the story clearer and easier to understand? _____

_____

_____

NARRATION 11

Name: _____

Date: _____

Two years ago, on spring break, I went to my friend's house. We took our bikes on this little path that goes into the woods. We cut across some fields. Then we stopped and had a picnic. We ate chips and drank some pop. We had a radio and we listened to some music. We sat and talked for a long time. It was getting really late so we had to leave. We took the path back to my friend's house. Then I had to hurry home so I wouldn't get in trouble.

NARRATION ELEMENTS

SETTING

CHARACTERS

TIME

EVENTS

  Beginning

  Ending

Was this story clear and easy to understand? _____
Why? _____

_____

_____

If the story was not clear, what could we do to make the story clearer and easier to understand? _____

_____

_____

NARRATION 12

Name: _____

Date: _____

One day, him and his friend went to the park. They saw these birds. They were magic birds, not regular birds. The birds said, "We will fly you someplace." They said, "Okay." So they were flying all around in the air. Then he got scared and wanted to get off. The birds stopped and they got off.

NARRATION ELEMENTS

SETTING

CHARACTERS

TIME

EVENTS

  Beginning

  Ending

Was this story clear and easy to understand? _____

Why? _____

_____

_____

If the story was not clear, what could we do to make the story clearer and easier to understand? _____

_____

_____

STORYBUILDING

NARRATION 13

Name: _____

Date: _____

Her mom took her at the zoo. She sees a monkey and she sees a giraffe. Now she went to a cage of lions. Now she comes to a place where a person sells balloons and stuff. Sometimes she sees elephants and stuff. She saw deers. Now she sees penguins. Then she went to a lake with ducks in it.

_____

NARRATION ELEMENTS

SETTING

CHARACTERS

TIME

EVENTS

  Beginning

  Ending

Was this story clear and easy to understand? _____

Why? _____

_____

_____

If the story was not clear, what could we do to make the story clearer and easier to understand? _____

_____

_____

NARRATION 14

In the summer, me and my friend, Mike, we were going out to my grandma's on a bike ride. My dad said it was going to rain, but we didn't really believe him so we went anyways. We got halfways out there and it started to rain, just sprinkling a little bit. We didn't think it would rain much more. We were just going up the hill and suddenly it was a downpour. I looked up into the sky and there was lightning. It came down and it zapped Mike right in the finger. He goes, "Ow, I got zapped by lightning" and I said, "Oh, geez! Let's get out of here." We rode up the hill and went all the way down the other side of the hill. It seemed just like hours to get down the hill because it was raining and thundering. Big crashes. We got down to a house and we stopped and went into their house to get out of the rain. It let up a bit so we went off again. Then my sister came and got us.

NARRATION ELEMENTS

Name: _____ Date: _____

Narration: _____

SETTING

CHARACTERS

TIME

EVENTS

Beginning

Ending

Was this story clear and easy to understand? _____

Why? _____

_____

_____

If the story was not clear, what could we do to make the story clearer and
easier to understand? _____

_____

_____

_____

STORYBUILDING

NARRATION 15

One time, last fall, my father and I and my two brothers went out to help plant trees at a farm. We were planting trees where one person would dig a hole and the other would put the tree in. They also had a machine that would dig the hole and plant the tree for you. We spent two hours working at one place, where we planted 50 trees in a field. Then we went down to another field by a creek. We planted trees there for a few hours. Then later we ate lunch and went back to planting. Afterwards, we went for a long hike in the woods. We went by another creek where we saw a few tadpoles and a couple of frogs. We saw many wild animals and many different trees, plants, and flowers. It would be fun to do this sort of thing again. I guess I really enjoyed it. It was hard work but it was fun too.

NARRATION ELEMENTS

Name: _____ Date: _____

Narration: _____

SETTING

CHARACTERS

TIME

EVENTS

   Beginning

   Ending

Was this story clear and easy to understand? _____
Why? _____
_____
_____

If the story was not clear, what could we do to make the story clearer and easier to understand? _____
_____
_____
_____

STORYBUILDING

NARRATION 16

Sally woke up one beautiful, sunny morning. Sally looked out her window and saw a beautiful rainbow. Sally had always heard stories that at the end of the rainbow there was a pot of gold. She knew the end of the rainbow was far away and that her parents would be upset if she went looking for the pot of gold. Sally had to make the decision whether she should go or should not go. Sally made the decision to go.

Sally left her home and walked for miles and miles trying to find the end of the rainbow. Unfortunately, she got lost in the woods. Sally didn't know where to go or what to do. She was very scared and upset. Night was coming. She sat by a tree and wondered what was going to happen. She wanted to go home. Soon, she fell asleep.

The next morning, Sally woke up. She was cold and wet. She wandered around the woods, trying to find her way home. She tried to remember how she had come the day before. Finally, her parents found her. Sally decided that she would never go out in the woods alone again.

NARRATION ELEMENTS

Name: _____ Date: _____

Narration: _____

SETTING

CHARACTERS

TIME

EVENTS

Beginning

Ending

Was this story clear and easy to understand? _____

Why? _____

_____

_____

If the story was not clear, what could we do to make the story clearer and easier to understand? _____

_____

_____

_____

NARRATION 17

There once was a little boy named Danny, who was 8 years old and he wanted to have a birthday party. He asked his mom and dad if he could and they said, "Yes." He didn't really know who to invite 'cause he really didn't have that many friends. But, he decided just to ask a few people that he knew and got along with. His parents said he could have a party anytime he wanted. So he decided to have it on the exact day of his birthday, August 4th. He told his parents what he really wanted for his birthday. He wanted to get a bicycle, but he didn't know if he would get it because money was tight and the bicycle he wanted was expensive.

The day finally came and it was a Saturday morning. He told his friends to come around noon. It was 12:00 and no one showed up. It came to be 1:00 and no one was there. His parents were helping him to not feel bad but he knew that his friends would not be coming.

He saw a big present in the corner of the house and he thought for sure that he was getting a bike from his mom and dad. He asked his parents if he could open the present and they told him to wait just a little bit longer. So he waited another hour.

Finally, some of his friends came. They said that they had been in a traffic jam and they were sorry that they were late. Danny opened all his presents and he did get a bicycle from his mom and dad. Then he was very happy.

NARRATION ELEMENTS

Name: _____ Date: _____

Narration: _____

SETTING

CHARACTERS

TIME

EVENTS

Beginning

Ending

Was this story clear and easy to understand? _____

Why? _____

_____

_____

If the story was not clear, what could we do to make the story clearer and easier to understand? _____

_____

_____

_____

NARRATION 18

There were these two kids who were going to visit their aunt. It was a boy and a girl. The girl was named Amanda and the boy was named Bill. They were riding on the train because an airplane was too expensive. It was Christmas vacation and their mom and dad were with them.

They were sitting on the train when they heard a lady scream. Bill and his dad went to see what it was. A man had stolen the lady's purse. Bill and his dad looked all around the train. They wanted to find the thief and return the woman's purse. They hoped the thief would try to steal something else so they could catch the thief. Then they saw a four- or five-year-old boy. A man came by and tried to get the little boy's money. Bill and his dad told the little boy not to give it to the man because he was the man that took the lady's purse. When the train stopped, Bill and his dad took the man to the police. The police said the man was a criminal. The police gave Bill and his dad a thousand dollar reward.

Now they had enough money to buy tickets for the airplane. So they went on a plane to visit their aunt.

NARRATION ELEMENTS

Name: _____ Date: _____

Narration: _____

SETTING

CHARACTERS

TIME

EVENTS

Beginning

Ending

Was this story clear and easy to understand? _____

Why? _____

_____

_____

If the story was not clear, what could we do to make the story clearer and easier to understand? _____

_____

_____

_____

NARRATION 19

There was this boy named Matt. He was the star of Memorial High's basketball team. He was 6'7" and the coach had one special play for him. It was an Alley Oop Dunk and they called it Number 9. One day they were playing a tough team and Matt came down hard on his ankle. He got injured and had to stay out for half the season. The coach told him, during that half the season he had to do something else to rest his ankle. Join a club or something. He joined this videotaping club, that taped all the basketball games the team played. At first he didn't want to 'cause he had to work with this really smart kid, and Matt just wanted his ankle to heal so he could play basketball. The guys on the team called this smart kid "Geek." But after Matt started to work with him, he really liked him. They had fun together, taping all the games. They'd go over the tape afterwards and see all the good and bad parts. They became good friends and did their homework together.

Then Matt got back on the basketball team. It was a play-off game and the coach said, "You can try out your ankle and if you don't feel right, you can come out and we'll put someone else in." The first play was Number 9 and Matt had to dunk it. He landed on the ankle and felt fine. They made it to the championship and Memorial High won the championship.

His friend stayed in the video club and whenever he had a chance, Matt would work with his new friend.

NARRATION ELEMENTS

Name: _____ Date: _____

Narration: _____

SETTING

CHARACTERS

TIME

EVENTS

  Beginning

  Ending

Was this story clear and easy to understand? _____

Why? _____

_____

_____

If the story was not clear, what could we do to make the story clearer and easier to understand? _____

_____

_____

_____

NARRATION 20

Once there was this boy. His name was Peter. He was a person that was good in sports and liked to talk to people. He could get along very well. Sometimes he wasn't as good at some things as other people were. He couldn't do his subjects as well in the classroom as other people could. He felt that he wasn't the same as other people. He would do good on his tests if he had a lot of time to study. When they had to answer questions in class, he didn't do as well. He would go to special classes about a half hour a day. He was in band and he could play just as well as anybody else could. Other people sometimes didn't want to make friends with Peter because they were thinking that he was different from them. He was worried about that when the new school year started because he wanted to have more friends.

Then a new person came to the school. Peter and the new boy decided to be friends and then the other kids would want to be their friends, too. They took the same classes and sat together at lunch. They liked each other. They had a lot in common. By the end of the school year, they were good friends and they had made some other friends, too. They had helped each other make new friends.

NARRATION ELEMENTS

Name: _____ Date: _____

Narration: _____

SETTING

CHARACTERS

TIME

EVENTS

Beginning

Ending

Was this story clear and easy to understand? _____

Why? _____

_____

_____

If the story was not clear, what could we do to make the story clearer and easier to understand? _____

_____

_____

_____

ANSWER KEY

NARRATION 1

SETTING: Not given but probably a kitchen
CHARACTERS: The narrator
TIME: Tomorrow
EVENTS:

Beginning:
1. The narrator is going to make Rice Krispies® bars.
2. Melt butter.
3. Add marshmallows to the melted butter.
4. Melt the marshmallows.
5. Stir the mixture.
6. Measure the Rice Krispies® and add to the pan.
7. Mix in the Rice Krispies®.
8. Put the Rice Krispies® mixture in a long cake pan.
9. Spread out the mixture.
10. Put the pan in the refrigerator.
11. When the mixture hardens, Mom cuts the bars.

Ending:
12. You eat them.

NARRATION 2

SETTING: In the car going to grandma's house
CHARACTERS: Mom, dad, the narrator, some deer
TIME: Thanksgiving
EVENTS:

Beginning:
1. Mom, dad, and the narrator were going to grandma's house on Thanksgiving.
2. A big deer ran in front of the car.
3. Dad stopped the car.
4. The deer ran into the woods.
5. They waited for a short while.
6. Two more deer ran across the road.

Ending:
7. Dad said there are many deer on that road.

NARRATION 3

SETTING: Minnesota
CHARACTERS: Mom, the dog, Peanut, the narrator
TIME: At night
EVENTS:

Beginning:
1. The narrator went camping in Minnesota with his/her family.
2. The dog Peanut went too.
3. Mom got up in the night to close the windows.
4. It was beginning to rain.

Ending:
5. The dog Peanut was sleeping in mom's sleeping bag when she looked in the bed.

NARRATION 4

SETTING: The gym
CHARACTERS: The cheerleaders, the kids, the coach
TIME: The basketball game days
EVENTS:

Beginning:
1. On basketball game days, there are pep rallies.
2. The cheerleaders go to the grades.
3. The kids cheer.
4. One class gets a stick thing.
5. Sometimes the coach talks.

Ending: Not given

NARRATION 5

SETTING: A show on TV
CHARACTERS: The characters were not explained
TIME: Not given
EVENTS:

Beginning:
1. There's a show on TV.
2. These guys were fighting.
3. There was a bomb which blew up a girl's car.
4. The police came.
5. One man ran away and the police chased him.
6. The man jumped in the water and began to swim away.
7. The police jumped in the water and caught him.

Ending: Not given

NARRATION 6

SETTING: A movie on TV
CHARACTERS: Monsters, a little girl, other people
TIME: Not given
EVENTS:

Beginning:
1. There was a movie with monsters on TV.
2. One monster was tall and green and he frightened the other people.
3. The little girl was lost.
4. The people thought the monster had the little girl.
5. The people looked for the little girl.
6. They went to where the monster lived.
7. The monster had the little girl.
8. The people and the little girl were crying.
9. The little girl liked the monster and wanted to stay with him.
10. When she went home, the little girl gave her doll to the monster.

Ending: 11. Now no one was afraid of the monster because he was nice.

NARRATION 7

SETTING: Jellystone, at mom's (Not explained well)
CHARACTERS: The narrator (Others are not explained)

TIME: After mom and dad divorced
EVENTS:

Beginning: 1. Mom and dad got divorced.
2. At's dad's house, they go to Jellystone where they swim, play golf, eat nachos, play games and shoot pool.
3. They buy things.
4. They go to their mom's.
5. Sometimes they don't go to their dad's.
6. Mom keeps them to go to school.

Ending: Not given

NARRATION 8

SETTING: A lake in Canada
CHARACTERS: The narrator, his dad
TIME: In the summer
EVENTS:

Beginning: 1. The narrator went fishing on a lake in Canada with his dad.
2. The lake was 90 square miles.
3. There were many bays and rivers attached to the lake.
4. They caught many fish.
5. The highlight of the trip was catching a 42 inch, 17 pound northern.
6. The head of the northern was mounted on a plaque, hanging in the room.

Ending: 7. They are going back next year.

NARRATION 9

SETTING: Not given
CHARACTERS: The narrator
TIME: Not given
EVENTS:

Beginning: 1. The narrator has collections.
2. The collections are little cars and seashells from the ocean.
3. There are many shells in the ocean.

Ending: Not given

NARRATION 10

SETTING: The pool
CHARACTERS: The narrator, Marvin, lifeguard
TIME: In the summer
EVENTS:

Beginning: 1. In the summer, the narrator was at the new pool.
2. Marvin, who is in another grade, pushed the narrator in the water.
3. The lifeguard didn't see it.
4. Then Marvin was pushed in the water.

Endng: Not given

NARRATION 11

SETTING: A friend's house
CHARACTERS: The narrator and a friend
TIME: Two years ago on spring break
EVENTS:

Beginning:
1. Two years ago on spring break, the narrator went to a friend's house.
2. They took their bikes on a path, in the woods, which cut across some fields.
3. They had a picnic with chips and pop.
4. They listened to music on the radio and talked.
5. It was getting late so they hurried back.

Ending:
6. The narrator had to hurry back to avoid trouble.

NARRATION 12

SETTING: At the park
CHARACTERS: The characters were not explained.
TIME: One day
EVENTS:

Beginning:
1. The narrator and his friend went to a park.
2. They saw some magical birds.
3. The birds offered to fly them someplace.
4. The children agreed.
5. They flew around.
6. One of the children became frightened and wanted to get off.
7. The birds stopped and they got off.

Ending: Not given

NARRATION 13

SETTING: The zoo
CHARACTERS: A girl, her mom
TIME: Not given
EVENTS:

Beginning:
1. A girl and her mom went to the zoo.
2. She saw a monkey, giraffes, and lions.
3. There was a person selling balloons.
4. The girl saw elephants, deer, and penguins.
5. There was a lake with ducks.

Ending: Not given

NARRATION 14

SETTING: Riding bikes to grandma's house
CHARACTERS: The narrator, a friend Mike
TIME: In the summer
EVENTS:

Beginning:
1. Two friends were going on a bike ride to grandma's house.

2. The narrator's dad told them it would rain, but they decided to go anyway.
3. Halfway there, it began to rain.
4. As they went up a hill, it began to rain very hard.
5. Lightning hit Mike in the finger.
6. They went up the hill and down the other side.
7. It continued to storm.
8. It seemed to take a long time to get down the hill.
9. They went into a house to get out of the rain.
10. The rain let up so they got on their bikes again.

Ending: 11. The narrator's sister picked them up.

NARRATION 15

SETTING: A farm
CHARACTERS: The narrator, his dad and two brothers
TIME: Last fall
EVENTS:

Beginning:
1. The narrator, his dad and two brothers helped plant trees on a farm.
2. One person would dig a hole and the other would put the tree in.
3. They also had a machine that would do this.
4. They worked for two hours and planted 50 trees.
5. They planted trees in another field by a creek for a few hours.
6. Then they ate lunch and went back to planting.
7. They took a long hike in the woods.
8. In a creek, there were tadpoles and frogs.
9. They saw many wild animals and different trees, plants, and flowers.

Ending: 10. It was hard work but fun and it would be fun to do this again.

NARRATION 16

SETTING: Sally's home, the woods
CHARACTERS: Sally
TIME: A day
EVENTS:

Beginning:
1. Sally woke up one morning and saw a beautiful rainbow.
2. Sally had heard there was a pot of gold at the end of the rainbow.
3. Sally knew her parents would be upset if she went looking for the gold but she decided to go.
4. Sally left home and walked for miles until she was lost.
5. Sally became scared and upset because she wanted to go home.
6. That night, Sally sat by a tree and fell asleep.
7. When Sally awakened the next morning, she was cold and wet.
8. Sally wandered around the woods, trying to find her way home.
9. Finally, her parents found her.

Ending: 10. Sally decided that she would never go into the woods alone again.

NARRATION 17

SETTING: Danny's house
CHARACTERS: Danny, his mom and dad, Danny's friends
TIME: Danny's birthday, Saturday, August 4th
EVENTS:

Beginning:
1. Danny was eight years old and wanted to have a birthday party.
2. Danny's parents agreed to let him have a party anytime he wanted.
3. Danny chose August 4, the date of his birthday.
4. He invited a few people he knew and got along with.
5. Danny told his parents he really wanted a bike.
6. Danny didn't know if he would get it because money was tight and the bike was expensive.
7. Danny told his friends to come at noon.
8. It was 12:00, then 1:00 and no one had arrived.
9. Danny thought his friends wouldn't be coming.
10. Danny wanted to open the big present in the corner but his parents told him to wait a little longer.
11. Danny waited another hour.
12. When his friends arrived, they said they had been in a traffic jam and were sorry they were late.
13. Then Danny opened his presents and he did receive a bike from his parents.

Ending:
14. Danny was very happy.

NARRATION 18

SETTING: On a train
CHARACTERS: Bill, Amanda, Mom, Dad, a lady, little boy, and a man
TIME: Christmas vacation
EVENTS:

Beginning:
1. Two kids, Bill and Amanda, were going to visit their aunt during Christmas vacation with their mom and dad.
2. They were riding on a train.
3. They heard a woman scream.
4. When Bill and his dad went to see what was happening, they learned that a woman's purse had been stolen.
5. Bill and his dad looked around the train.
6. They wanted to find the thief and return the purse.
7. They saw a four- or five-year-old boy.
8. A man tried to take the little boy's money.
9. Bill and his dad told the little boy not to give his money to the man since he had stolen the woman's purse.
10. When the train stopped, Bill and his dad took the man to the police.
11. The man was a criminal.
12. The police gave them a $1000.00 reward.

Ending:
13. They used the reward money to buy airplane tickets to visit their aunt.

NARRATION 19

SETTING: Memorial High School
CHARACTERS: Matt, coach, the smart kid
TIME: Basketball season
EVENTS:

Beginning:
1. Matt, who was 6'7", was the star of the Memorial High School basketball team.
2. The coach designed a special play for Matt called the Alley Oop Dunk, Number 9.
3. Matt hurt his ankle in a game and had to miss half the season.
4. At the coach's suggestion, Matt joined a videotaping club which taped the basketball games.
5. Matt didn't want to tape the games because he had to work with this smart kid the others called "Geek."
6. Matt and the smart kid became friends and did their homework together.
7. When Matt got back on the team, there was a play-off game and the coach sent Matt in to try out his ankle.
8. On the first play, Number 9, Matt dunked the ball.
9. Matt's ankle felt fine.
10. Memorial High won the championship.

Ending:
11. Matt and the smart kid remained friends.

NARRATION 20

SETTING: School
CHARACTERS: Peter and a new boy
TIME: School year
EVENTS:

Beginning:
1. Peter was a boy who was good at sports and liked to talk to people.
2. He had trouble doing his school work.
3. He felt he was different from other people.
4. If he had time to study, he could do well on his tests.
5. He had trouble answering questions in class.
6. Peter went to special classes for a half hour a day.
7. He was in band and played very well.
8. Some people didn't want to make friends with Peter because they thought he was too different.
9. Peter was worried about that when school started.
10. Then a new person arrived at school.
11. Peter and the new boy decided to be friends.
12. Peter and the new boy had classes together and ate their lunch together.
13. They liked each other.
14. They were good friends and had made other friends.

Ending:
15. They had helped each other make new friends.

STORY GRAMMAR ELEMENTS
STUDENT COPY

Name: _____   Date: _____

Title of story: _Narration 16_

Source: _____

What is the setting? _The woods_

Who are the characters? _Sally, her parents_

When did this occur? _One day_

What happened first? _Sally saw a rainbow._

What happened next? _Sally went into the woods looking for the pot of gold at the end of the rainbow._

Was this event caused by the first event? How? _Yes, Sally saw the rainbow and went searching for the pot of gold she had heard was at the end of the rainbow._

What is the goal? _Goal 1 - To find the pot of gold_
Goal 2 - To find her way home again

What is the plan to reach this goal? _____
Plan for Goal 1 - Looking in the woods
Plan for Goal 2 - Trying to find her way back home

How was the plan attempted? _Goal 1 - Sally left home and walked for many miles trying to find the end of the rainbow. Goal 2 - Sally tried to remember which way she had come._

What was the result? _Sally was very frightened and upset. She was lost in the woods._

How did it end? _Sally's parents found her. Sally decided that she would never go out in the woods alone again._

Using this form, retell the story.

STORY GRAMMAR ELEMENTS
STUDENT COPY

Name: _____ Date: _____

Title of story: *Narration 17* _____

Source: _____

What is the setting? *Danny's house* _____

Who are the characters? *Danny, his mom and dad* _____
_____

When did this occur? *Danny's birthday, Saturday, August 4th* ___

What happened first? *Danny wanted to have a birthday party on his birthday,*
August 4th. _____

What happened next? *Danny's parents agreed to let him have the birthday party*
when he asked them. _____
_____

Was this event caused by the first event? How? *Yes, Danny wanted to have a*
party and his parents agreed. _____
_____
_____
_____

What is the goal? *Danny wanted to have a birthday party with his friends.* ___

What is the plan to reach this goal? *Danny told his friends to come at noon for*
the party. _____

How was the plan attempted? *Not given.* _____
_____
_____

What was the result? *Danny's friends arrived late because they were in a traffic jam.*
Danny opened his presents. He did get a bike from his parents. ___
_____

How did it end? *Danny was very happy.* _____
_____
_____

Using this form, retell the story.

STORYBUILDING

STORY GRAMMAR ELEMENTS
STUDENT COPY

Name: _____ Date: _____

Title of story: _Narration 18_

Source: _____

What is the setting? _A train._

Who are the characters? _Amanda, Bill, their parents, a lady, little boy and man on the train._

When did this occur? _Christmas vacation_

What happened first? _Bill, Amanda and their parents were sitting on the train when they heard a woman scream._

What happened next? _When Bill and his dad went to see what was wrong, they found out that a man had stolen the woman's purse._

Was this event caused by the first event? How? _Yes, the woman screamed because her purse had been stolen. Hearing the scream, Bill and his dad went to investigate._

What is the goal? _To find the thief and return the woman's purse_

What is the plan to reach this goal? _Bill and his dad looked around the train. They hoped they would see the thief trying to steal money from someone else._

How was the plan attempted? _As they looked around the train, they spotted the thief trying to take money from a little boy. They told the little boy to keep his money. When the train stopped, Bill and his dad took the man to the police._

What was the result? _The police said the man was a criminal and gave Bill and his dad a $1,000.00 reward._

How did it end? _Now, Bill, Amanda and their parents had enough money to buy plane tickets to visit their aunt._

Using this form, retell the story.

STORYBUILDING

STORY GRAMMAR ELEMENTS
STUDENT COPY

Name: _____ Date: _____

Title of story: *Narration 19* _____

Source: _____

What is the setting? *Memorial High School* _____

Who are the characters? *Matt, the basketball coach, a smart kid* _____
_____

When did this occur? *During basketball season* _____

What happened first? *Matt injured his ankle and had to miss half the season.*
_____

What happened next? *The coach told Matt to join a club. Matt joined a videotaping* *club and became friends with a smart student.*

Was this event caused by the first event? How? *Yes, Matt joined the club* *because be had injured his ankle and couldn't play basketball.*
_____
_____
_____

What is the goal? *For Matt's ankle to heal so he can play basketball.*
_____

What is the plan to reach this goal? *The coach told Matt to do something else while* *the ankle heals.*
_____

How was the plan attempted? *Matt joined a videotaping club and became good* *friends with a very smart student. They taped games together and did their homework* *together.*
_____

What was the result? *When Matt's ankle healed, he got back on the team. Memorial* *High School then won the championship.*
_____

How did it end? *Matt and the smart student remained friends. Matt would work with* *his new friend whenever he had a chance.*
_____
_____

Using this form, retell the story.

STORYBUILDING

STORY GRAMMAR ELEMENTS
STUDENT COPY

Name: _____   Date: _____

Title of story: _Narration 20_

Source: _____

What is the setting? _School_

Who are the characters? _Peter, a new boy_

_____

When did this occur? _During the school year_

What happened first? _Peter was good at sports and liked people but he didn't do well in class unless he had a lot of time to study._

What happened next? _Peter went to a special class each day. Some people didn't want to be friends with Peter because they thought he was different from them._

_____

Was this event caused by the first event? How? _Yes, Peter went to special classes because he didn't do well in class. Since he didn't do well in school, some people thought he was different and didn't want to be his friend._

_____

What is the goal? _Peter wanted to have more friends._

What is the plan to reach this goal? _Peter and a new boy decided to be friends so that the other kids would want to be friends with them._

How was the plan attempted? _Peter and the new student took the same classes and ate lunch together._

What was the result? _Peter and the new boy helped each other make more friends._

How did it end? _Peter and the new student were good friends and they had made more friends._

Using this form, retell the story.

STORYBUILDING

GENERALIZATION

At this point, the students have had experience producing, discussing, and analyzing oral narratives. The students have made frequent use of the narrative elements forms. Knowledge of story schema should be internalized by the child as well as an understanding of how the story elements fit together to produce a clear, well-formed story.

The fourth phase of the *STORYBUILDING* program involves the generalizing and condensing of these newly acquired skills. A suggested, sample IEP goal is listed below. Through the use of assignments, these narrative skills are generalized to other settings (e.g., classroom, home) and to other modes of communication (e.g., written language). Too often, skills that are mastered in therapy activities are not evident in the child's conversations with peers and adults. One reason for this failure to generalize may be the language and learning disabled students' deficiency in recognizing the similarity of situations in which existing knowledge should be applied (Kamhi, 1988). Therefore, the focus of this section is to provide activities that will extend this knowledge of story schema to other applications.

Story schema and narration knowledge provide an organizational strategy that the language/learning disabled student can use throughout his/her day. Using brainstorming techniques, discuss with the students other situations in which they may be called upon to tell a story or relate a personal event. Some of these situations could be sharing time, creative and experiential writing assignments, book reports, etc. Point out the similiarities of the skills needed in these situations to extend story schema usage.

To ensure continued use and development of these narrative skills, the speech-language pathologist will need to create additional narrative activities. Generalization should be stressed throughout the speech-language therapy sessions.

Included in this *Generalization* section are the following:

1. Listener Letter
2. Book Report Format
3. Creative Writing Outline
4. Experiential Writing Outline

SAMPLE I.E.P. GOAL

The student will be able to generalize narrative skills to other settings and other modes of communication, with 90% or greater accuracy.

BOOK REPORTS

Book reports done in the upper elementary grades are frequently story reformulation tasks with evaluative comments added. These summaries may be oral or written. Knowledge of story schema provides an excellent format for organizing story content in a book report. Application of story schema knowledge to content areas helps to generalize these skills.

DIRECTIONS: With an individual student or a small group, assign a book to be read. The students may select their own books, but the adult may need to supervise the selection. A book that corresponds to the student's content area provides additional background in that content area and makes the activity more meaningful. Some examples of this would be: short biographies of early American presidents for U.S. history, tales of daring rescues for health class, and fictionalized accounts of scientific discoveries for science class. For students who are poor readers, the "Books on Tape" series may be used. Instruct the students to read the book and then prepare a report on that book, using the form on the following page. As a transition, the *Story Frame* form presented on page 66 of the *Practice* section may also be used. These completed forms may then serve as the basis for a written report or an oral report. With some prior discussion with the classroom teacher, this report may be presented to the class or turned into the teacher for extra credit.

Name: _____

Date: _____

BOOK REPORT FORMAT

TITLE OF BOOK: _____

AUTHOR OF BOOK: _____

The setting of this story was _____

_____

The characters in the story were _____

_____

_____

The time the story occurred was _____

_____

A brief summary of the <u>important</u> events would include _____

_____

_____

_____

In this book, I liked_____

_____

In this book, I didn't like _____

_____

Would you suggest this book to a friend? Why? _____

_____

If you could, what would you change about this book? _____

_____

_____

STORYBUILDING

WRITTEN NARRATIVES

Creative and experiential stories are required of students from the first grade on through middle and high school years. Unfortunately, many language/learning disabled students possess poorly developed written language skills. The organizational problems that are evident in the oral narratives of language/learning disabled students are also apparent in their written language. The stories of inexperienced and poor writers may contain no central theme and story parts may be missing, unclear, presented out of sequence, or unrelated (Hall, 1981). Application of story schema and narrative knowledge to written language can enhance the student's creative and experiential writing.

For students who are unable to make the transition from oral to written narratives, an intermediate step may be necessary. The student can formulate an oral narrative and relate this narration onto an audio-cassette tape. Using the pause button, the students can then transcribe this story onto paper.

Included on the following pages are forms to facilitate the students' construction of creative and experiential stories. The *Creative Writing Outline* is written in the future tense, since the student will be outlining a story he/she is about to write. The *Experiential Writing Outline* is written in the present tense, as the student will be writing about an event that is occurring or has already occurred. This verb tense shift was used to assist the student in developing written narrations.

CREATIVE WRITING

DIRECTIONS: Instruct the student to write a creative story using the form on the following page. Students for whom the mechanics of writing preclude the completion of this assignment may be allowed to tell the story to a tape recorder or a transcriber. Once again, the incorporation of content area subject matter is beneficial for the generalization of skills. The students may be asked to write about life as an early American settler, or to create an original story using five words from their spelling word list. Have the students fill in the basic form with the necessary story content information. The completed form may be used as an outline for the actual story writing. The questions on the bottom are provided as a means of guiding metanarrative awareness. These stories may then be turned into the classroom teacher as part of a daily writing assignment, as a special project, or as extra credit work.

Name: _____

Date: _____

CREATIVE WRITING OUTLINE

TITLE OF STORY: _____

TOPIC OF STORY: _____

The setting of my story will be _____

_____

The characters in my story will be _____

_____

The time my story will take place is _____

_____

The first event that will happen will be _____

_____

_____

The next events that happen will be _____

_____

_____

The ending of my story will be _____

_____

After you have finished writing your story, read it over and answer these questions.

Am I being clear?
Is the information in the story organized well?
Do all the sentences relate to the topic of the story?
Does the reader know what I am trying to say?

EXPERIENTIAL WRITING

DIRECTIONS: Instruct the student to write a story based on a personal experience. Topics could include trips, holiday celebrations, summer vacations, family activities, school events, etc. Once again, students for whom the mechanics of writing preclude the completion of this assignment may be allowed to tell the story to a tape recorder or a transcriber. Prior to writing the story, the student will need to determine if the story will be written as an event that has already occurred or will be written as the student relives the experience and writes about the events as they are happening. Indicate to the student that events from the past need to be written using past tense verb inflections, while events as they occur require present progressive verb inflectional endings. Using the outline on the next page, fill in the necessary information. The completed form may then be used as an outline for the actual story writing. The questions on the bottom of the page are provided as a means of guiding metanarrative awareness.

Name: _____

Date: _____

EXPERIENTIAL WRITING OUTLINE

TITLE OF STORY: _____

TOPIC OF STORY: _____

The setting of my story is _____

_____

The characters in my story are _____

_____

The time of my story is _____

_____

The first event is _____

_____

_____

The next events are _____

_____

_____

The ending of my story is _____

_____

After you have finished writing your story, read it over and answer these questions.

Am I being clear?

Is the information in the story organized well?

Do all the sentences relate to the topic of the story?

Does the reader know what I am trying to say?

STORYBUILDING

BIBLIOGRAPHY

Applebee, A. *The Child's Concept of Story.* University of Chicago Press, Chicago, IL, 1978.

Applebee, A. and Langer, J. Instructional scaffolding: Reading and writing as natural language activities. *Language Arts* 60(2): 168-175, 1983.

Ault, R. *Children's Cognitive Development.* Oxford University Press, New York, 1977.

Fowler, G. Developing comprehension skills in primary students through the use of story frames. *Reading Teacher* 36, 176-179, 1982.

Glenn, C. and Stein, N. *Syntactic Structures and Real World Themes in Stories Generated by Children.* Technical report. University of Illinois, Center for the Study of Reading, Urbana, IL, 1980.

Gmeiner Heinrich, A. *Language and Literacy: The Role of the Speech-Language Pathologist.* Paper presented at the Wisconsin Speech Language and Hearing Association Convention. Delevan, WI, April, 1989.

Hall, J. *Evaluating and Improving Written Expression: A Practical Guide for Teachers.* Allyn & Bacon, Inc. Boston, MA, 1981.

Hedburg, N. and Stoel-Gammon, C. Narrative analysis: Clinical procedures. *Topics in Language Disorders* 7(1): 58-69, 1986.

Johnston, J. Narratives: A new look at communication problems in older language-disordered children. *Language, Speech, and Hearing Services in Schools* 13(3): 144-155, 1982.

Kamhi, A. A reconceptualization of generalization and generalization problems. *Language, Speech, and Hearing Services in Schools* 19(3): 304-313, 1988.

Kayser, H. Speech and language assessment of Spanish-English speaking children. *Language, Speech, and Hearing Services in Schools* 20(3): 226-244, 1989.

Kemper, S. and Edwards, L. Children's expression of causality and their construction of narratives. *Topics in Language Disorders* 7(1): 11-20, 1986.

Larson, V. and McKinley, N. *Communication Assessment and Intervention Strategies For Adolescents.* Thinking Publications, Eau Claire, WI, 1987.

Norris, J. and Brunig, R. Cohesion in the narratives of good and poor readers. *Journal of Speech and Hearing Disorders* 53(4): 416-424, 1988.

Page, J. and Stewart, S. Story grammar skills in school-age children. *Topics in Language Disorders* 5(2): 16-30, 1985.

Roth, F. Oral narrative abilities of learning-disabled students. *Topics in Language Disorders* 7(1): 21-30, 1986.

Roth, F. and Spekman, N. Narrative disclosure: Spontaneously generated stories of learning-disabled and normally achieving students. *Journal of Speech and Hearing Disorders* 51(1): 8-23, 1986.

Roth, F. and Spekman, N. *Story Grammar Analysis of Narratives Produced by Learning Disabled and Normally Achieving Students.* Paper presented at the Symposium on Research in Child Language Disorders, Madison, WI. June, 1985.

Scott, C. A perspective on the evaluation of school children's narratives, *Language, Speech, and Hearing Services in Schools* 19(1): 67-82, 1988.

Simon, C. *Communication Skills and Classroom Success: Assessment of Language-Learning Disabled Students.* College-Hill Press, San Diego, CA, 1985.

Stein, N. and Glenn, C. An analysis of story comprehension in elementary school children. In: R. Freedle (ed.), *New Directions in Discourse Processing.* Erlbaum, Hillsdale, NJ, 1979.

Stephens, I. *Normal Language Development: Ages 9-19.* Paper presented at the American Speech-Language-Hearing Association Convention, New Orleans, LA, November, 1987.

Sutton-Smith, B. and Heath, S. Paradigms of pretense. *The Quarterly Newsletter of the Laboratory of Comparative Human Cognition* 3, 41-45, 1981.

Van Dongen, R. and Westby, C. Building the narrative mode of thought through children's literature. *Topics in Language Disorders* 7(1):70-83, 1986.

Westby, C. *Cultural Variations in Storytelling.* Paper presented at the American Speech-Language-Hearing Association Convention. St. Louis, MO, November, 1989.

Westby, C. Learning to talk-talking to learn: Oral-literate language differences. In: C. Simon (ed.), *Communication Skills and Classroom Success: Therapy Methodologies for Language-Learning Disabled Students.* Little Brown/College-Hill Press, San Diego, CA, 1985.

Westby, C. Development of narrative language abilities. In: G. Wallach and K. Butler (eds.), *Language Learning Disabilities in School-Age Children.* Williams and Wilkins, Baltimore, MD, 1984.